THE DEVIL IN GOD'S LAND
An Eritrean Play

THE DEVIL IN GOD'S LAND
An Eritrean Play

Bereket Habte Selassie

MKUKI NA NYOTA
DAR–ES–SALAAM

PUBLISHED BY
Mkuki na Nyota Publishers Ltd
Nyerere Road, Quality Plaza Building
P. O. Box 4246
Dar es Salaam, Tanzania
www.mkukinanyota.com
publish@mkukinanyota.com

© Bereket Habte Selassie 2011

First Edition 2011

ISBN 978 9987 08 161 5

CONTENTS

PREFACE

This is a play based on contemporary history of a particular place and people. This kind of particular history provides a point of departure for the writer, as the raw material, so to speak, but is not itself exactly history. Just as a block of wood from a felled mahogany tree provides the sculptor with the raw material from which he/she fashions a work of art (wood sculpture) a novel or play based on historical reality uses material but transcends it in fashioning the story. Like most works of literature based on reality and using that reality, this play involves critical evaluation of historic events, expressly or impliedly making value judgments. In making such judgments, the proverbial poetic license would exonerate the writer from blame.

The historical background of the play is a new nation emerging from a bloody war of liberation; and a population faced with a government that betrayed its trust. The principal protagonist is engaged in self-flagellation for having taken part in an infamous resolution by the National Assembly, of which he is a high-ranking member. His wife, who was also his comrade-in-arms during the liberation struggle, is puzzled and tries to understand and help him but he seems beyond help. The nation's capital city is filled with rumors of a bankrupt and servile National Assembly and foreboding of worst things to come. Events and places, such as the killing and funeral of a freedom fighter at the cemetery of Enda Mariam, as well as secret meetings of veterans of the war at the same cemetery, provide the context and venue for acting out some of the tensions between the protagonists and antagonists, the latter being the defenders of the regime. The cemetery also symbolically represents the nexus between the fallen heroes and the living freedom fighters now facing the dilemma of choosing between a future of dishonor within the governing party, or a second liberation which demands sacrifice. Hence the thematic head-note of Act Four, *Sacrifice and Redemption*.

Funerals and weddings are important events in Eritrean tradition, as in much of Africa. And the place where a person is buried concerns not only belief systems of a people, that is to say spiritual matters; but it also involves social and cultural values and issues that bind communities. When a person dies he or she joins the ancestors. In pre-Christian and pre-Islamic times, the burial ground was invariably graced with trees and considered sacred ground. In Eritrea, with the advent of the post-liberation "heroic" era the burial ground of heroes tegadelti was delineated from that of "ordinary mortals" called gabar. Where a person is buried thus becomes a mark of distinction, defining a person's place in society even in death. Hence the dramatic conflict occurring at the beginning of Act Three of the play.

The protagonists of this play—all heroic freedom fighters—are caught on the horns of a dilemma. The feel they have been betrayed, their lifetime struggle and sacrifice reduced to naught. The principal protagonist, Senai, is a composite of a tegadalai and a muhur (educated scholar) who sacrificed career and even family for the sake of the cause of national liberation. On the other hand, there are the antagonists typified by the ambitious security chief, Teklu and the party apparatchik, Delta, who measure their success by the smile of the Boss and the reward of position in the party and government. They will do anything and everything the Boss tells them to do. In their world, failure is not permissible and in order to maintain their positions they are prepared to do anything. As Teklu, the fearsome Security Chief, says to one of his subordinates in driving home the point about ends justifying means, including torture:

"...I intend to keep my head on my shoulders. Do you get my drift?

Subordinate: Yes sir. We have to extract the necessary information with the use of any means.

Teklu: If in the process some unfortunate soul has to have his nails plucked out, or if he becomes impotent, or paralyzed below the waist, tough luck. That is the price paid for keeping our heads on our shoulders, Clear?

Subordinate: Perfectly clear sir.

The genesis of this play is as intriguing as its subject matter. I started writing it under the title *Simbrat Semblia* (The Blemish of the Assembly). The reference was the passing of the infamous resolution mentioned above, passed in February 2002, condemning eleven of its members and charging them with treason at the instigation of an unelected president. The present title under which the play is published is much more compelling in terms of representation of the tragic condition of the country. For the rest I leave to the reader to navigate through the intricacies of the story. I have added a phrase at the head of each act of the play, a phrase denoting the underlying theme of each Act. This departure from traditional play writing must be the academic in me, and I trust that there will be no hue and cry because of it. If there is, so be it.

Bereket Habte Selassie

Chapel Hill, North Carolina, November 2011.

DEDICATION

This book is dedicated to the youth of Eritrea who are destined to save OUR wounded nation, and reclaim the betrayed values of justices, democracy and the rule of law.

DRAMATIS PERSONAE
(In the order of their appearance)

DR. SENAI
A High-ranking Party Official and Dissenter

ASTER
Senai's wife

YIKALO
Their son, a university student

ASKALU
Their daughter, a high school graduate

YONAS
Yikalo's friend and fellow student

SABA
Yonas' girl friend

FOUR OF SENAI'S FELLOW DISSENTERS
Members of an underground movement, using assumed names

DESTA
Top Party official

IDRIS
Businessman

GIRMAI
Senai's friend and colleague

KIFLE
Senai's friend on visit from America where he lives

TEKLU
Security Chief

MANNA
Teklu's prisoner

AWETASH
Manna's wife

ANDU
Teklu's deputy

CASHIER AT THE CAFÉ ADULIS
Senai's suspected paramour

ZEGONFO II
An emaciated old character thought to be mad but also a soothsayer and incarnation of an ancient national hero

SISTER DELORES
A nun at the catholic church and convent

ACT ONE

A Fateful Decision

SCENE ONE

[An Evening in Asmara in early February.

It is after six o'clock in the evening. The streets of Asmara are unusually deserted. A strange quiet has descended upon this beautiful Italianate city, which has known better days. The Cafés and bars are practically empty. The cashier in the Café Adulis, a very attractive woman in her early-thirties, is nervously watching the few remaining clients, presumably wishing they would go home. She is anxious to go home to her family. One client whom she watches with great interest rises from his seat and comes forward to pay. To her great surprise, he does not respond to her usual pleasantries; he just hands her the money, which is out of character.]

SENAI	Keep the change and buy your kids some candy.
CASHIER	Thank you Dr. Senai. Are you all right?
SENAI	Yes, why do you ask?
CASHIER	I don't know; you seem quiet and distracted. We are used to your cheerful manner, which cheers everybody.
SENAI	*[Glum]* These are not cheerful times, are they?
	[As Senai was about to leave the Café, a man dressed as a bahtawi makes a dramatic entry and takes Senai by the arm, pulling him to the middle of the café and leans on his shoulders. Then he blows a whistle to the

amazement and amusement of the customers. There is a general murmur and some who knew him say, "It is Zegonfo II." His bahtawi dress consists of a long, yellow traditional costume, a netsela wrapped around it, a leather satchel hanging from his shoulders diagonally across his chest, a rope tied around his waist and a black priestly cloth cap. His long beard shows a touch of gray, and his emaciated figure and manner of walking and talking give him an aura of authority. He commands attention in this place where he was least expected.]

"Your Majesty," cries one customer.

ZEGONFO II	Wrong! Falso! You should address me as reverend. I am not of this world; my kingdom is not of this world. So you are wrong to address me as Your Majesty. What is your name?
CUSTOMER	Araia
ZEGONFO II	Araia, go and write "falso" fifty times on the blackboard.
ARAIA	But there is no blackboard here, Zegye.
ZEGNFO II	What did we teach you at the trenches? Be creative. Where there is no blackboard, make one. Didn't we do it in Sahel? Eh, didn't we?
ARAIA	If you say so, Zegye.
ZEGONFO II	Wrong again. Not if I say so, it is so. Don't be timid. Stand up for your rights and fight! Being timid is how he has got his boots on your necks. *[Turning to Senai who is mildly amused but also somewhat embarrassed and was anxious to be released from this temporary "detention."]* Isn't that right comrade Senai? You should know, your neck is under his boots.
ANOTHER CUSTOMER	Be careful Zegye, the police will arrest you.
ZEGONFO II	Arrest me! How can they arrest a dead man? Don't you know that a bahtawi is not of this world? *[A mischievous smile brightens his handsome face, exhibiting decaying teeth]*. But...aha! I shall rise from the ashes...We shall all rise from the ashes, I and the other martyrs.
CUSTOMER	Are you a martyr then?
ZEGONFO II	*[Ignoring the interruption]* When we made a commitment, we renounced the things that are of this world. We were martyred before dying; I was a walking dead. That makes me immune to their power.

THIRD CUSTOMER	*[Addressing a friend nearby]* This Zegonfo may be mad, but there is method in his madness.
FOURTH CUSTOMER	All right Mr. Polonius, where is the method?
THIRD CUSTOMER	His immunity. None of us could say what he has been saying about the tyrant and get away with it.
FOURTH CUSTOMER	But none of us is willing to pay the price of losing his mind. Which is better, losing your mind or your freedom?
THIRD CUSTOMER	You miss my point. This man is not mad, he is pretending to be mad. Do you remember the other Zegonfo of earlier days? He was play-acting all the time, while pretending to be crazy, and sending a message at a time when there was no freedom of expression. Even the Eritrean police under Haile Selassie's government who were sympathetic to our cause, played along by making believe that he was mad. That was a subtle method born of desperation. In fact that is the reason why people started calling this one Zegonfo II. People create their means of struggle and invent heroes where there may be none.
FOURTH CUSTOMER	You may be right, but I need convincing, we'll see.
	[Meanwhile Zegonfo II engages Senai in a quiet dialogue and then blows his whistle to draw the attention of the customers].
ZEGONFO II	*[Pointing to Senai]* This is a good man. He was my good comrade-in-arms. We saw many battles together. Tell me Senai, when are you going to be true to yourself? Have you forgotten your vows to the martyrs? Can you honor your vows while in the cruel embrace of the powerful?
FOURTH CUSTOMER	Tell us what trust has been betrayed, Zegye.
ZEGONFO II	*[Ignoring the interruption]* But the weak shall be strong. Fools shall be wise. The dead shall rise and those who think they are alive are really dead. No one who has betrayed his trust can be alive. *[Turning his gaze to the fourth customer who interrupted him]*. You think you are alive, but you just proved you are not. If you don't know the betrayed trust of the martyrs, you are not living; you are a zombie. He has turned you all into walking zombies.
SENAI	Zegye, I must go now, some people are waiting for me at home. Okay old buddy?

ZEGONFO II	*[Hugging Senai]* Okay comrade. God be with you. Beware of the evil ones—they are all around you. They smile and pretend to be on your side, but are sharpening their daggers to stab you in the back. Beware! Beware!
SENAI	Okay, I will be careful. Goodbye Zegye.
	[Senai leaves the café and walks towards his car. He gets into his car and waits a long time before he starts the engine, as the cashier watches him with obvious concern.]
	As he starts his car to go home, he exclaims "Assemblea nazionale di merda!"

SCENE TWO

[In Dr. Senai's home a few days later

Dr. Senai Embaie is sitting curled up in a sofa in the small dining room of his house that he uses as his office. He is lost in thought—thought of the extraordinary events of the past few days, of what happened in the meetings of the National Assembly. Occasionally he utters exclamations as if he is responding to an inner voice. His wife, Aster, who is preparing dinner for the family and a couple of her children's friends—university students— left the kitchen door ajar on purpose so that she hears him, and as his soliloquy continues her worries increase. She could not wait any longer and decides to join him.]

ASTER	Are you all right?
SENAI	*[Startled]* Oh! Yes, I am all right.
ASTER	I have been hesitating to say this because I was not sure if it was just a passing thing.
SENAI	What are you talking about? Say what?
ASTER	Well, these last four days you have been speaking in your dreams. You keep repeating the same phrases in your sleep. And now you are talking to yourself, as if I didn't exist. I have been worried and I am still worried. You repeat the same words every night. What is happening? I mean, I know you have been having important meetings; it has been all over the media, after all. But you must know, this time people don't care any more. They have given up hope. People are saying that man forced you to pass those resolutions that we heard on the radio.

SENAI	What people are you talking about?
ASTER	People in the hotel where I work, for instance. Do you think everybody is afraid of him. They may not shout it from the rooftops, but they talk among themselves in hushed voices. They are saying many things. They are saying that the man has gone off the deep end. Why, he even
SENAI	[Angry and in an impatient tone] Stop it, you are giving it more weight than it deserves.
ASTER	What do you mean, what am I giving more weight to?
SENAI	You know very well what I mean.
ASTER	No, I don't. Perhaps you can tell me.
SENAI	What is there to tell?
ASTER	I am telling you I do not know because you keep everything to yourself. Party matters you say, or government secrets. Have you ever thought of the consequences of what you are doing? Why can't you share with your wife what you have been doing? You must know that what you do today will one day affect me and our children. It will come back to haunt all of us.
SENAI	[To himself] You are telling me!
	[Encouraged by his remark, she decides to challenge him more forcefully. She raises her voice, standing up and continues facing him down.]
ASTER	For heaven's sake be yourself, for once! That man does not care a cent about the rest of you, and you all do whatever he orders you to do. You behave as if he owns you. He may own your pockets but he does not own your souls, you know. Why are you people acting like cattle being taken to the slaughterhouse? Why can't you protest? What has happened to Eritrea's manhood? And why do you hide everything from me? But now what you hide from me, what you hide during the day, comes out in your sleep, in nightmares. You have been having nightmares and I am scared. Talk to me. I am worried sick and I can't take it any more. I...[She chokes and sits down in one of the other sofas and begins to sob in uncontrollable fits].
SENAI	You don't seem to understand. I am under stress myself and might even flip off like him, if I don't do something about this growing tension inside me. The bastard has pulled the wool over our eyes. It is time to be counted

among those who have arisen to rectify the situation before it is too late.

[Senai has already begun to feel the moral weight of her challenging words. Her words brought to the surface the frustration and sense of impotence that has been simmering below. He gets up and puts his coat on[.

ASTER   Please Senai, be careful. Think of us. Think of your children.

SENAI   I will, I will. Now I must go, I will be late. Don't wait for me.

[He walks out and disappears into the night].

SCENE THREE

A Dinner Conversation

[Four young people, two men and two women, are at home in the residence of Dr. Senai and Aster, alternating their place of conversation between the dinner table and the living room. One of the men, Yikalo, is their oldest son. He is 21 years old and attending the University of Asmara. One of the women, Askalu, aged 18, is their daughter and has just been ordered to go to do service in Sawa. The other two are their friends, Yonas, aged 21, a University student, and Saba, aged 20, his girl fiend who has just come back from doing service in Sawa and is enrolled to study in the University.]

ASTER   *[Calling her daughter from the kitchen]*
                Askalu, what time are your guests coming?

ASKALU   *[In the bathroom combing her long black hair]*
                Any minute now.

                The bell rings followed by a knock on the door.

ASTER   O, *Dio mio!* They are here already, what time is it? Go and open the door.

ASKALU   I will, mother, I will. Why are you so nervous? I have not known you to be like this.

ASTER   *[Quietly to herself]* How can you? You don't know what I am going through, you innocent child! And you don't know what is in store for us all! *Dio ci protegga!*

ASKALU   *[Opening the door]* Sabina! Yoni! Come in, come in. *[she kisses them both on the cheeks].* Come in and let's sit in the living room till dinner is served. *[Shouting]* Mammina, they are here.

ASTER	*[Comes out of the kitchen smiling, removes her apron and stretches her hand to greet them]* Hello...and welcome. I have heard so much about you.
YONAS	Good things, I hope.
ASTER	Nothing but good. Please sit down, make yourself at home, like it is your house. Dinner will be served soon. Senait, offer them something to drink. I will be back in a moment.
YONAS	Can we help you?
ASTER	No thanks, everything is ready and I will join you shortly.
SABA	You have such a nice and warm house.
ASTER	Thank you. We got it last year, after years of waiting. There was a long waiting list and the government bureaucracy is glacial, *Dio Mio*.
SABA	And the rent?
ASTER	It used to be reasonable. But they are now asking for a sum that we could not afford if we only depended on Senai's miserable government salary.
ASKALU	We'll do okay, *Mammina*. Besides, think of the thousands of other *tegadelti* who had no such luck. I mean if papa had not been a member of the Party's inner circle would we have got this house? Of course not, so count your blessings, as Maria Emma used to tell us in the convent.
YONAS	You were in the convent?
ASKALU	Yes I was, for over ten years, and came back here to join my family two years after liberation. Alas! I was not old enough to vote in the referendum.
	[Surprised, Saba and Yonas exchange glances and look at Aster. They cannot hide their surprise].
ASTER	I had to leave her in the care of Catholic nuns who belong to an Order of Sisters where I was educated when I was young.
YONAS	Where is that?
ASTER	In Milan, Italy. I was taken to Italy when I was young and went to school there. Then I joined the liberation struggle, and when I was in my sixth month of pregnancy carrying Askalu, I was given leave to go to Italy for the delivery because I had problems when I gave birth to Yikalo in the Field, three years earlier.

ASKALU	And so, she left me in the hands of the good nuns and came back to Sahel to fight. Is that heroic or what!
SABA	It must have been a difficult decision.
ASKALU	The most difficult decision I had to face in my life.
	Enter Yikalo with two bags, one filled with bananas, the other with oranges.
YIKALO	Sorry I am late. Aster, here are my humble offerings.
ASTER	Good God! Where did you get the money to buy all this? *[Turning to the guests]* Everything has become so expensive—*governo ladro!*
ASKALU	Mother, stop blaming the government. You know that they are doing their best. Without their intervention, things would become more expensive. *[The guests look at each other, surprised].*
YIKALO	That is what they tell you at the *Higdef* seminars.
ASKALU	That's the truth. You and mamma used to tell me so many good things about *Higdef* when I returned from Italy.
ASTER	Correction. Not *higdef*. I used to tell you about the EPLF. *[Contrite that she expressed her feelings about the government in front of strangers]* Anyway, that exclamation just came out of me. It must be my Italian education. The Italians blame the government even when it rains. *[Laughter].* Don't take it too seriously
ASKALU	But mother, there is no difference between *higdef* and EPLF.
ASTER	To you may be, dear child, but to me there is a world of difference. But we are boring our guests. Let's eat.
YONAS	No, far from boring us, this is instructive for those of us who did not share in the Sahel experience. What about Dr. Senai? Where is he?
ASTER	He had to attend a meeting. He sends his apologies and he will meet you some other time.
	[They all move to the dinning room and take their assigned seats, with Aster sitting at the head table, Yikalo to her right, Askalu to her left, and the guests sitting opposite each other. The food consisting of spaghetti, TSebHi Derho and Taita is on the table.]
Aster	Please serve yourselves. No need for ceremonies. Eat what the house offers which is not much but in these times... But before we eat, Askalu will say grace.

ASKALU	Bless us O Lord, and these thy gifts which we are about to receive from thy bounty in Jesus' name, Amen. *[They say "Amen" in unison and begin to eat in silence].*
SABA	Why Askalu, you are full of surprises; I didn't know you were conversant with religious matters.
ASKALU	It is all thanks to Mother. She saw to it that I was placed in the right institutions that say grace all the time.
YONAS	Woizero Aster, was there any problem for religious people in Sahel?
ASTER	At first, yes and we prayed silently. But eventually, they relaxed the unwritten rules.
YONAS	And did you experience any problems when you first joined the Front? By the way, I am curious to know and Yikalo could not tell me for sure when you joined the EPLF.
ASTER	I joined the ELF, not the EPLF, at first, in early 1977.
YONAS	Why did you move from one Front to the other?
ASTER	It is a long story. Have you heard of the group called *Falul?*
YONAS	Yes, of course. Were you a member of *Falul?*
ASTER	Yes.
YONAS	I thought *Falul* was a Marxist-oriented group that did not see eye-to-eye with the leadership of *Jebha.*
ASTER	It was a mixed group representing various tendencies, but the Marxist faction was not dominant... *[After a brief silence]* You are not eating. You must eat, we can talk later after the meal.
SABA	Yes, Yonni, you talk too much and you are exhausting our hostess with all these questions.
ASTER	No, not at all. His questions are pertinent, and I don't mind answering them. But you must eat first.
	They move to the living room. A large coffee pot and cups are placed on a tray.
YIKALO	*[Pointing to a photograph hanging from the wall, of a smiling handsome man with a moustache and high forehead]* Do you know who that man is, my friend?
YONAS	*[Rising and getting closer to the picture]* The face looks familiar, but I confess I don't know the man.

YIKALO	That is Ibrahim Afa. My father was in his unit for several years and talks about him all the time. Ibrahim was his role model as a freedom fighter.
YONAS	*[Excited]* Really? Sabina, come and look, it is the martyr, Ibrahim Afa, one of the great heroes of Eritrea.
SABA	Yonni, I know who Ibrahim Afa was. Everyone knows who Ibrahim Afa was. Those who knew him speak of him with such reverence and love you feel as if you knew him. And some people resent that. *[The two young men look at each other and at Saba slyly].*
YONAS	Yes, but does everyone know how he died? *[He throws a sly glance at Aster, gazes her with intense curiosity, then turns to Askalu. He is now sure that she is a Higdef supporter].*
ASKALU	As far as we know, he was killed in action. By all accounts he was universally liked and admired. I was told that everyone was shocked when it was announced at the Second Congress of the EPLF that he had been killed in action.
YONAS	Everyone except the EPLF leaders who kept his death a secret for over two years. And was he killed in action?
SABA	*[Holding her ground and getting angrier]* They had to keep it a secret so as not to affect the morale of the *tegadelti,* can't you understand?
YONAS	Well, there are all kind of stories told about his death and I am curious to know the truth, that's all.
ASKALU	Stories? You mean rumors that he was assassinated? I have heard them, we all have heard them, haven't we Yikalo? I mean it is all nonsense. It is enemy propaganda.
YIKALO	I wouldn't be too sure about that. I am keeping an open mind, until the full story of the incident is told. Aster, are you listening to the conversation?
ASTER	*[From the kitchen where she was depositing the plates and rinsing them.]* I will be with you in a minute. *[Coming to join the rest]* What have you been talking about?
YIKALO	Yonni has been quizzing us about the circumstances of Ibrahim Afa's death.
ASTER	It is best to leave that subject to history, in fairness to all concerned.

ASKALU	*[Exclaiming]* The judgment of Solomon! I am proud of you Mammina.
YIKALO	Not quite. Aster is being diplomatic.
ASTER	No, I am not, I am being fair and sensible. There is no proof one way or the other. So, why not leave it to the judgment of history.
YONAS	Speaking of history, has anyone written the history of Ibrahim Afa and other martyrs?
ASTER	To my knowledge, there has been no writing, and what has been written is not proper history. It is what they call hagiography, which is one sided with exaggerated claims favoring people now in power. I am afraid we have to wait for some time before the true history is written.
YONAS	While you are at it, I wonder if you could clear something for me. Some people claim that our leaders deliberately sent thousands of Falul units to futile battles and thus to unnecessary death in the battle for Massawa in 1977. Since you were a member of Falul, can you shed any light on that claim?
ASKALU	There you go again, repeating hostile propaganda.
YONAS	*[Showing signs of irritation]* Askalu, I am only asking a question that has been repeated by many and I want to know the truth. Are you afraid of the truth? *[Askalu bows her head, shaking her head in disbelief]*. Woizero Aster, you be the judge, am I asking the wrong question?
ASTER	There is nothing wrong with asking questions in search of the truth. We need that. In fact that is what has been missing here for a long time. We used to ask hard questions during the struggle, you know. It is only in recent years that we have been muzzled or we have imposed self-censorship. But I will repeat what I said with regard to Ibrahim Afa's manner of death. I would say again that we have to leave it to history. The truth will come out sooner or later. You can't suppress truth forever.
YIKALO	As far as I am concerned, we are distorting our priorities. Although I believe that military heroes like Ibrahim Afa should be given their place of honor, this mystique of *tegadalai* and military heroes encourages militarism which leads to wars and other irrational and harmful activities that are destructive.

SABA	I agree with Yikalo entirely. The arrogant behavior of some of the commanders in Sawa and in the war fronts that I observed is an aspect of militarism. Women in particular who are under the command of such people are vulnerable and subject to rape and other forms of degradation.
ASKALU	Are you speaking from personal experience, Saba?
SABA	Definitely.
	[Everyone turns towards Saba who is almost in tears and gets up].
ASTER	Are you alright Saba?
SABA	[With a quivering voice] Yes, I am alright. May I use the bathroom?
ASTER	Of course. It is the second door to the left.
	[She gets up and walks with Saba half of the way. and returns to sit with the others at the same time watching the reactions of the others. Saba enters the bathroom and closes the door behind her as the others keep quiet for a moment, puzzled by Saba's sudden emotional behavior. Aster returns to her seat and observes the reactions of the others].
YONAS	[Attempting to change the subject and turning towards Askalu] Asku, are you still planning to go to Sawa, depite your good chances of entering Asmara University?
ASKALU	Yes I am. Actually, I can't wait to get out there.
YONAS	Why are you anxious to go?
ASKALU	To serve, just as you have served
	[Saba returns smiling with embarrassment and apologizes]
SABA	I am sorry, I shouldn't have been so emotional.
ASTER	Nonsense, you should sometimes to let it out. We have been socialized to suppress our feelings and it is harmful. So don't apologize.
SABA	Did I miss anything important while I was wiping my tears? [She giggles. She has a very appealing giggle which Yonas has always found captivating].
ASTER	Yonas was asking Askalu if she is planning to go to Sawa and she replied that she can't wait to go out there. [Saba reacts with a bitter laughter].

SABA	I wish I had the advantage that you have now. I wish I had had someone who had been to Sawa and who could have told me what it meant to be a woman serving in Sawa, what went on there.
YONAS	*[Emboldened by Sabas words]* Askalu, what does it take to disabuse you of the romantic ideas you have about our leaders? Do you know what happens to a beautiful woman like you once a general or colonel in charge takes fancy on her?
ASKALU	I don't know what you are talking about.
YONAS	Then listen to what Saba will tell you, based on her experience. *[He turns to Saba, and everyone turns to her. But Saba shakes her head and declines to follow his suggestion to tell her story]*.
SABA	No, not now. I don't feel like talking about it. I will tell Askalu when we are alone, if she wants to listen.
ASTER	I have heard all kinds of horror stories about what goes on in Sawa. But frankly, I think it is exaggerated and used for propaganda purposes by critics of the government. While there are a number of issues on which I can criticize the government, I don't think it is fair to our armed forces to assume that they are abusing our daughters left, right and center. If they are engaged in such abuse, I will be the first to condemn them outright.
YIKALO	Aster is right in a sense, I mean we have to be fair and find out for sure whether the claims of abuse are true.
YONAS	How can we when the institution that can do that best, a free press, is gagged and its editors and reporters banished or detained?
YIKALO	I know, Yoni, I am a journalism major after all, and the leader of our university students union is also detained and held for months without charge. But why can't we organize ourselves in cells and find out from participants in the Sawa service what goes on there? What we need is a clandestine organization to make systematic and determined effort to find out exactly what goes on in Sawa and elsewhere on the war front.
YONAS	Easier said than done. How can we organize when the secret police are everywhere spying on us?
ASKALU	*[No longer able to control herself]* That's ridiculous. You have fallen victim to hostile propaganda. I have never been spied on or confronted by any secret police.

YIKALO	Perhaps that is because they believe you to be on their side, and you seem to be solidly on their side. That's why we are trying to disabuse you of the romantic hold the Party has on you.
ASKALU	Romantic hold! I believe in the PFDJ and you used to sing their praise too, a short while ago.
YIKALO	Ah, but I have learnt more about them. You know, you live and learn. If you don't learn as a result of tragic events, what can one make of you? *[After a brief and pregnant pause]*. The difference between you and me, dear sister, is that I keep an open mind and learn. I wish you would, for once, listen to your elders.
	[Askalu is visibly angry and was about to answer her brother but Saba intervenes].
SABA	Are you still planning to go to Sawa, then?
ASKALU	Yes I am.
SABA	Then you and I need to have a long, heart-to-heart talk. Believe me, it will be as much for my as for your benefit. At least, I will be happier for helping some one else avoid the perils I faced.
ASTER	*[Who really does not want Saba to go to Sawa, but is afraid to say so, is pleased with Saba's offer]* Well that is a good idea. Why don't you two set up an appointment? Perhaps, Saba, you could join us for lunch this coming weekend.
SABA	I would be happy to come, thank you. Just the two of us, Asku, okay?
ASKALU	Okay, but don't expect me to change my mind. Besides, I am under an obligation to do service, and there is no way out of this obligation even if I wanted to. Of course, as you know even if you receive the highest grades in the university entrance exam, you are no longer exempted. But the bottom line is I want to go, I want to do this service. You people have done your service, now let me do mine.
YONAS	It is not the service that we are against, it is the abuse in the name of national service. All we are asking you to do is to listen to the voice of those who have experienced the abuse. You would be surprised, believe me Saba, we are only concerned with your welfare. And by the way, there is always a way out if you pull the right strings.

ASKALU	[Her controlled anger exploding into a loud voice that shakes even the unflappable Yikalo] Don't talk nonesense. I am sure you are repeating the lies of the critics of the government. I know what I want, I know what I am doing and I can take care of myself!
YIKALO	He only meant to help, Saba, why are you acting this way?
ASKALU	What do you mean?
YIKALO	You are so edgy today? I have never seen you act like this.
	[Askalu bolts from her seat to her bedroom followed by her worried mother. Utterly confused and fearing that he was the cause of Askalu's distress, Yonas rises as though he could help Aster console Askalu. Saba also rises and the two lovers begin to walk towards the door. Yikalo rises to stop them and bids them sit down.]
YIKALO	Now what do you think you are doing? You are not thinking of leaving, are you?
YONAS	Well maybe if we left you and your mother could console her and reason with her. I just wish there were something I could do. I caused all this.
YIKALO	No you did not.
YONAS	Oh but I did. I was the one who said we must save her from the PFDJ.
YIKALO	Yonas, I am telling you, you are wrong. I know my sister. She doesn't take offense that easily. Besides we were all trying to help her.
SABA	Yikalo is right, Yonas. Our aim was to save her from suffering the same fate that some of us unfortunate ones have suffered. But I want to know what made her fly into a temper tantrum like that. I want to be her sister and help her, but I can't help her if I can't tell her the truth.
YIKALO.	You will. She will be alright. You see, Askalu grew up away from her family and I believe that this had an effect on her emotional development. She is a wonderful human being, kind and generous. But she is on the naïve side.
SABA	That is all the more reason why we must save her from the clutches of the scheming cadres of PFDJ.

YIKALO	Saba is right, these people are users. They suck you like a lemon and throw you away as soon as the juice is finished. Askalu is a very trusting person. She takes things and people at face value. And she has practically no experience of going out with men. No romantic involvement with anybody yet. The bastards can entrap her through the use of some *wedini* con-man.
YONAS	If they haven't already, you mean. She is a beautiful woman, anyone would fall for her. I suspect they must have already laid the trap for her.
YIKALO	That may be but she has had no romantic entanglement with anybody. If she had, she would have shown the usual signs.
SABA	You'd be surprised how much we women can dissimulate. And, despite the lack of experience, Askalu is not a baby.
YIKALO	Maybe you are right. But I would have known somehow or other. We are very close, despite the temper tantrum that you just saw. She tells me almost everything.
YONAS	Does she tell you about their meetings at the PFDJ youth organization?
YIKALO	Not in details. She has often tried to get me to resume membership and when I resist, she does not press the matter. She respects my right to refuse to belong to any organization. She has a strong sense of privacy and space.
SABA	In that case she will be crushed in Sawa. The first thing they do is to rob you of your sense of privacy, your self-respect.
YONAS	I am not being the devil's advocate; far be it from me. But I have been reading lately about the history of military organizations. And the control of private space is the first law of military drill.
YIKALO	But we are civilians and our fight for freedom must include freedom of private space and the ability to say no.
	Aster comes back with Askalu, smiling with some embarrassment.
ASTER	Askalu has something to say. Go on Askalu.
ASKALU	I am sorry I flew into a rage. I don't want you to feel I do this all the time.

SABA	[Rushing to hug her] It is quite alright Asku, we all do that sometimes. [They sit side by side]. And you and I will have a real talk, soon. Okay?
ASKALU	Okay.

SCENE FOUR

[Massawa in early February, a Special Party Meeting at the Red Sea Club

It is the best time of the year in Massawa, this enchanting ancient port city. The Red Sea Club, which is headquartered in the Red Sea Hotel, recently built and owned by the governing Party, lies at the northern end of the city. The members of this exclusive elite club are mostly various VIPs—high-raking government and Party officials, their special guests, army officers and prominent businessmen, whose number has been shrinking these days. From earlier days when prominent businessmen were sought out by ingratiating Party agents promising them profitable partnerships, they have now dwindled in number, as the party takes over their businesses one after one another. They cannot competer. It is widely believed by owners of private businesses, large and small, that the Party business entities do not pay taxes and other dues and they can rely on government support, including insider information, to drive private businesses out of the market.

This evening, three high-ranking Party officials and two security officers are meeting to chart out a strategy for the expansion of the Party business. They are seated on expensive leather armchairs bought from Italy. The armchairs are arranged in a semicircle with Desta sitting at the center. Spare chairs are arranged in front and on two sides of the center. An item on the meeting agenda that proved controversial is the business of a certain prominent businessman, one of the few remaining competitors. Attending the meeting, with great reluctance but keeping his feelings to himself, is our friend, Senai who is one of the three party officials. The meeting and its agenda are under the control of Desta Aregai, a top dog and trusted right hand man of the Boss.]

DESTA	So, we are all clear about the agenda of today. Are there any items that anyone wants to add?
SENAI	Excuse me for asking, and no offence meant, but what are our comrades from the security department doing at this meeting which concerns Party economic affairs?
DESTA	Somehow, I expected you to ask that question. The best way I can answer that is simply "because the Boss ordered it." That is the bottom line. Would that be enough, or shall I elaborate?

SENAI	Again, no offence meant but yes, please do elaborate. Did the Boss give reason for his order?
DESTA	No, he did not; he does not have to. You should know that, Senai.
SENAI	No, I didn't know that. I work on the principle that there is reason for everything. I also work on the assumption that comrade Chairman is a reasonable man, a reason-loving man.
DESTA	[Laughing, as he always does when cornered] Of course, of course. Well, the matter will be made clear when we reach item number three on the agenda, the matter of Idris Musa. And by the way, the Boss has asked that our security comrades are to attend our future meetings when there are issues of criminal offence suspected or under investigation. Any thing else, Dr. Senai?
SENAI	No, not now.
DESTA	Good, so we can proceed. We will begin with the first item, then. As you all know, our Party's economic program is based on our Macro Policy which came out of the genius of our great leader.
SENAI	Actually, it came out of a number of sources and it became a guiding economic ideology which the Ministers repeated like a mantra. We all repeated the mantra even though we didn't understand it.
DESTA	Why Senai, I am surprised. You, a doctor of political economy from one of the best Italian Universities, don't understand Macro Policy?
SENAI	Perhaps you can expound it for me someday.
DESTA	[Hiding his annoyance by his inimitable laughter] You are just teasing us ignoramus nonentities, and I'll let it pass. Let me just repeat for the sake of a common understanding the three principal pillars self-reliance, export-oriented growth, and competition in a free market is based on the Macro Policy. All the progress our country has made in the last ten years shows how correct the Party's policy is. Now, our opponents have made wild accusations that our Party has monopolized the economy of the country. We know that this is wicked propaganda. These agents of foreign interests who have lost their stranglehold on the economy and the chance of exploiting the labor of our suffering masses, can say what they want, but the fact remains, our people have never had it so good. And they can't bear to see this,

as we can tell from some of their statements. *[Turns towards the first security officer]*

FIRST
SECURITY OFFICER
We have proof of their connection with foreign interests who finance the publication of the hostile news being propagated against our government.

SENAI
What kind of proof?

FIRST
SECURITY OFFICER
Telephone conversations that we taped over the last three years, plus reports of our informants from inside their secret organizations.

SENAI
You mean you bugged their telephones?

FIRST
SECURITY OFFICER
Let's say we have ways of tracing their illegal activities. By the way, we are not the only ones who trace illegal activities by using electronic surveillance. The Israelis do it, the Americans do it. Even the British, with their talk of the Rule of Law, do it.

SENAI
In the first place, I don't think you are right when you say that they all do it. Some may do it in exceptional circumstances. In any case, even the evidence that they obtain this way in exceptional circumstances is not admissible in a court of law. In the second place, if the Americans go astray why do we have to follow them? Not all that the West does is right, and much that it does is not good. We should be able to pick and choose the good and leave out the bad. They didn't invent the rule of law. The rule of law is innate to humanity, although it has been violated by tyrants. Now, see what you have done. You have provoked me to launch into one of my favorite subjects.

DESTA
I know, Senai. That is one of your weaknesses. But let me tell you what we think of the law. The law is and has always been the weapon of the strong who use it to advance their basic policy. The policy of ancient Rome was the preservation of the Roman Empire. Anybody who stood against that policy was not tolerated. Those who opposed it were dealt with severely. The policy of the British Empire followed a similar line, and so does that of the emerging American empire. And we in our little corner of the world have our own little policy. One of them is the maintenance of our unity and territorial integrity. Anyone who dares to go against that policy has to be dealt with severely, rule of law or no rule

of law. Hence our stringent measures including the detention of he defeatists and foreign collaborators.

SENAI I still insist on evidence. Again, this is not the exclusive property of the Americans or the British. In our own traditional law, no one was convicted without being confronted with his accuser and without being given a chance to defend himself. If he is not capable to defend himself able lawyers came to his rescue. So you see, the application of the concept of the rule of law, as guaranteed in our yet unimplemented Constitution is an aspect of natural law, having nothing to do with the Americans or the Europeans.

DESTA What is the relevance of all this?

SENAI Even the European colonial rulers recognized this rule and allowed the native colonized people to apply it. I have serious questions about the way we are handling the rule of law and I will continue to speak within the Party. After all, we are supposed to have internal Party democracy. I think I have said enough about the rule of law. Now what about our economic policy?

DESTA In the economic sphere, our policy is that until the private sector is developed and can be trusted as having the correct business ethic, we shall continue to play a major role in the country's economy and our business concerns will grow accordingly.

SENAI Is there a time limit?

DESTA There you go again, Senai. You and your obsession with time. It is the disease of our so called educated classes.

FIRST SECURITY OFFICER As a member of the so-called educated classes, I suggest an amendment to your statement. I say the chattering classes, because not all the educated people are the same. I mean you can't classify Senai, here with the SOBs that have been maligning our government, can you?

DESTA You are right, Teklu. Senai, I apologize for lumping you together with the SOBs. I didn't mean to; it just came out of me. [He bursts into his characteristic laughter which some say is one reason why the Boss likes about him, in addition to his blind loyalty].

SENAI [Trying to imitate Desta's laughter without success] Don't worry, I am not easily offended. Only people with a fragile ego are easily offended. Wouldn't you say

	so, Teklu, on the strength of your vast knowledge of psychology? *[Teklu winces and shifts in his chair, trying to control his temper].*
DESTA	*[Anxious to avoid another fight between the two who have never liked each other]* Comrades, comrades! Gentlemen, please, control yourselves. We are straying from the agenda of our meeting. Now where were we?
SECOND SECURITY OFFICER	You were explaining the Party's economic policy.
DESTA	Yes, thank you Andu. Now take the construction business, for example. No country that has any sense of self-respect should depend on other countries for the materials it needs for the construction industry. The United States built its industry on that principle, on the principle that it must be self-sufficient on food and on housing needs, the two essential areas in any people's life. All building materials for housing as well as other types of construction must be procured from the home market. The guiding principle is, don't consume what you can't produce. And if you produce what you can't consume, look for outside markets.
SENAI	Are you saying that we are in the same situation in which the United States was two hundred years ago?
DESTA	No, not exactly, but the principle applies universally. And if you have been following the speeches of our great leader, we can apply the principle by studying the example of the Asian Tigers, especially Singapore.
SENAI	And what is the relevance of all this to the business at hand, to our agenda?
DESTA	The relevance lies in the fact that the cornerstone of our economic policy is self reliance which is exemplified by our Party business enterprises. Now one of the reasons why we have been encroaching on the private businesses is that they do not share our philosophy and, therefore, constitute a threat to the health and progress of our country and society. When we come to consider item number three of the agenda, we will see the application of the policy of business take-over in accordance with the policy of self reliance.
DESTA	Now we come to the main reason why we are gathered here today. Dr. Senai, perhaps you have not been aware of the fact that Idris Musa, one of the few remaining principal competitors to our Party's business enterprises

is also connected with the dissident group that has lately been sowing dissention in the ranks of our Party, putting the country's unity and stability at risk.

SENAI	I was not aware of that.
DESTA	Well, you will have ample opportunity today.
SENAI	How so?
DESTA	*[Turning to one of the security officers]* Is Idris here?
SECOND SECURITY OFFICER	Yes he is. He is waiting in the special lobby. *[Smirking]* I don't think he knows what is in store for him.
DESTA	Bring him in.

[The second security officer springs to his feet and swaggers towards the door. Senai scans the faces of the other participants, struggles with his conscience and decides he has to play along until the right time...Idris comes in, greets everybody as if he was joining a friendly card game, and sits in the empty chair, facing Desta].

IDRIS	Senai, long time no see. Have you been traveling abroad, on the local government small industry project we talked about?
SENAI	No, I have just been busy.
DESTA	Idris, we have called you to make a business proposition. We don't need to waste time, so I'll come straight to the point. *[He looks him straight in the eye and his jaw muscles stiffen]*. We want to acquire seventy-five percent interest in your import export and your construction businesses. We can discuss the terms of this acquisition and the management and other administrative questions.
IDRIS	I'll give you my answer in two words, Desta: Not interested.
DESTA	And I'll give you my answer to that anwer in four words You have no choice.

[Desta, assisted by the security officers, goes into detail concerning Idris' business, hinting at the shady nature of some of his business deals as well as political activities. Although not shaken, Idris knows that he is at a disadvantage, because they repeatedly hint at his collaboration with a prominent, recently detained democratic activist. In his defense, Idris makes reference to his past service to the cause. He keeps reminding his tormentors that he was an active supporter of the

liberation struggle to which he gave enormous amount of money and other forms of assistance. They laugh at this, leaving him to wonder whether he was dreaming, because he remembers how some of them used to fawn on him and flatter him during the struggle when they used to come asking for assistance in the Sudan and in Europe].

IDRIS   You must be out of your minds. How can I relinquish seventy-five percent of my shares when I built this company from nothing and let you in because I believed in the cause?

DESTA   Because if you don't, you may lose everything; that is why. Do you get it now?

IDRIS   Desta, how can you say this to me? Have you forgotten what I used to do for you when you were a destitute refugee in the Sudan? Have you all forgotten what I contributed to the cause all those years?

DESTA   No, we have not forgotten. Nor have we forgotten that you used to exploit young girls for your business, offering them for hire to Sudanese officials in exchange for favors they did for you to make your millions. You think we didn't know? Ha...ha...ha...ha! We kept a record of everything. So don't give us this pious talk about helping me and the cause. For you, the cause is your millions. Remember, the hand of the *Sewra* is long and you should be grateful that we did nothing to you for the crimes you committed against our sisters. Now that is the reality.

IDRIS   Crimes? Crimes! Ya Allah! Listen to him! Look who is talking! Now you listen to me. I didn't kill or torture my comrades. I didn't waste millions of the people's money. I didn't gallop around the world, staying in five star hotels on the people's money, dispersing gifts left right and center. I didn't pick and choose the prettiest girls and spend night after night in clubs on the people's money. I didn't steal other people's businesses in the name of the people. Did I? Now, you tell me.

[Startled by this unexpected pluck, Desta looks at the others who are equally startled. He tries to deflect the frontal attack of Idris.]

DESTA   Come on Idris, now be sensible and take our offer and stop this foolish talk. The offer is on the table, take it or leave it.

IDRIS	I have heard you, I am not deaf; you don't have to repeat what you have already said loud and clear. I know that if I don't take it I will lose all my business. I also know why you are pushing me, squeezing me out of my business ventures. Your boss has told you about our attempts to counsel tolerance, reconciliation and good governance. He has not forgiven me for initiating the move. He ordered you to squeeze me didn't he?
ANOTHER PARTY MAN	Look Idris, don't take this too personally. There are a lot of other businessmen who are cooperating and enjoying the benefits of joint ventures. This is the best approach to business partnership between the public and private sector in a creative way. Why, even the World Bank has been applauding it.
IDRIS	*Dahya TaKhud al World Bank!* To hell with them! How do they know what is good for the country? If they approve of what is happening here with all this official theft of people's money and property, then they are part of our problem, that's all.
TEKLU	Mind what you say, old man, this may land you in real trouble.
IDRIS	Damn your impudence! Who are you to tell me what to mind and what not to mind, you hoodlum!
TEKLU	We have been meaning to take you in anyway; this is a convenient excuse, you son of a bitch! *[He takes over from the second security officer and slaps Idris repeatedly. Again, Senai intervenes. Blood starts coming out of Idris' mouth, as the others watch thunder-struck and fascinated. Even Senai had stood paralyzed before he intervened, and Idris looks at him with puzzlement, groaning from his injury].*
IDRIS	Is this the payoff for what I did for my country? You too, Senai! Are you in league with them? *[Senai tries to smile encouragingly as if to say, "I am sorry" but Idris just shakes his head in disbelief].*
DESTA	Hey, Idris, you brought it upon yourself. You called Teklu a hoodlum and he slapped you in retaliation. You gave him a nasty header; the rest was a logical consequence of your own foolish talk. Fair is fair.
IDRIS	Never mind. We thought we were different from the rest of the continent. But we are all the same. Dictators are all the same. Senai, who was it who said, "Revolutions

have never lightened the burden of tyranny they have only shifted it to another shoulder"?

TEKLU

We thank you for your wise words. *[Turning to the second security officer]* Take him away. There is a limousine outside, waiting to take His Excellency Al Said Idris to his special headquarters. *[They all laugh, except Senai who is mortified by the incident and by Idris' fate. He tries to imagine himself in his place. Idris manages a wry smile, as he is led away by the second security officer who pulls him by he scruff of the neck].*

SENAI

Tell me Desta, why is he being led away like a criminal?

DESTA

Because he is a criminal.

SENAI

Come on! Just because he was involved in a scuffle? That could happen to any one of us?

DESTA

No, Senai. Didn't you here what we said earlier, before he was brought in. This man is in league with the defeatists and conspirators who wanted to overthrow our leader.

SENAI

Just a curiosity, would he have gone free, had he agreed to the business proposition?

DESTA

Maybe today, but it would be a matter of time before he would be picked up. We have enough incriminating evidence, as you heard. *[A knock at the door and a young man comes in with a visiting card and gives it to Desta who reads it and turns to Senai].* It is for you, Senai. You do remember, don't you, that at the meeting of the National Assembly, last week, the report of the Party clearly indicated that there are traitors in our midst who have been conspiring against our Party and leader. They have been having secret deals with our enemies.

SENAI

Of course I remember. You also remember, don't you, that I did ask for clear evidence to prove the allegation. The Chairman overruled my request and ignored me repeatedly when I raised my hand to speak.

DESTA

Yes, I do remember, and I wondered why you kept insisting on evidence when the rest of us took the word of our leader on its face value. Why insist on evidence when everybody went along with the report and the Resolution the Assembly. This is not America. This is Eritrea; we are a Third World country.

SENAI

Do you mean to say that we are to be judged by lower standards of evidentiary rule than Americans because we are Africans? Well, you have already heard what I think of that. I will spare you another tirade. But I tremble for the fate of our Party and our country.

[The telephone rings and Desta motions to Senai to take a seat. Senai complies and Desta picks the phone, sitting on his Manager's chair behind the desk].

DESTA

Hallo! *[He springs to his feet and the smile disappears from his face, replaced by an anxious frown. His voice, which had an ironic edge as he was speaking to Senai, loses its playfulness as he utters the first word in response to the caller]* . Yes.......Yes, we did make the offer to him. *[He waits for the voice at the other end to finish]* We made the offer strictly in accordance with your instruction.....Yes, he rejected the offer arrogantly. He also was insulting to our comrades....As a result he was taken in handcuffs....Yes, I will report in person.

[He hangs the receiver and a mixture of relief and anxiety drain his chubby face, despite his attempt to hide it from Senai's curious eyes].

SENAI

The Boss?

DESTA

Yes...He does not seem to be happy with the result.

SENAI

What did he expect?

DESTA

I don't know. Sometimes I wonder if anyone knows what he really wants. It is so confusing.

SENAI

Okay, see you in Asmara.

[Senai leaves first and Desta settles on his desk chair, and picks up the phone to start and make phone calls.]

ACT TWO

Veteran's Dilemma

SCENE ONE

[One month later, on a star-lit, warm Saturday evening in mid March, a secret meeting is about to begin at Inda Mariam Cemetery. Enda Mariam cemetery is a peaceful haven for the weary and the desperate. It is also a refuge for vagrants and, occasionally, for fugitives. Although one gets an eerie feeling sitting among the dead, it is one of those places that just feels safe. The deathly quiet induces in the spirit a strange sense of security. But it was not for this quality that the five veteran freedom fighters chose it as their meeting place for this, their hazardous venture. Senai and another leading participant had come ahead of the others and are quietly chatting while waiting for the others to arrive.]

SENAI	You know, I feel one with those of our comrades who are interred here. I feel a sense of community with them. We have sacrificed so much to help liberate our country, and I feel betrayed. Although I am alive, I feel close to the dead in my sense of loss. Don't you?
OTHER PARTICPANT	I do.
SENAI	It is a crippling feeling. It leads one to despair and regret. Was it worth squandering our youth for and sacrificing our families? What does the future hold for us and for the country?
OTHER PARTICIPANT	Aren't we meeting here to provide an answer to that question?
SENAI	Imagine, the older generation expected their children to reap the benefits of the liberation, but their children have been cheated of their heritage. They are wasting away in the trenches.

OTHER PARTICIPANT	And he has created this division between *Yikaalo* and *Warsai*— Divide and rule.
SENAI	Yes, that is devilish. We have a duty to rectify this division before it gets out of hand.
OTHER PARTICIPANT	I'll drink to that!
	[The others arrive and the meeting begins. The convenor is the one who had arrived earlier with Senai.]
CONVENOR	*[Clearing his throat].* Friends, and fellow conspirators, welcome to this crucial meeting. You'll have noticed I did not call you comrades. The word comrade in the past defined our common destiny, our dedication to a cause greater than ourselves as well as a thrilling adventure in the face of possible death that could strike any moment. A comrade was a brother nearer than a blood brother, and a sister closer than a blood sister. But we have discovered that the idea was used and exploited by those whom we trusted and who used it to gain power.
A PARTICIPANT	Why did you welcome us as conspirators? They are the conspirators, not we. Those who betrayed us, who have high-jacked our revolution and our democracy, are the conspirators.
CONVENOR	Hey! We can use a bit of humor even in these bad times, I think. I just want to say that we are all taking a huge risk in undertaking this venture.
CONVENOR	Yes, of course. We are aware of the risks involved in what we are doing. There is always the risk of being discovered and of what would happen to us, if we are exposed. Our freedom and maybe our lives and those of our loved ones may be at risk. We are embarking upon this enterprise in full knowledge of its dangers. Is there any doubt on this? *[They all shake their heads grimly and vigorously].*
	We will adopt fictitious names, then we will swear an oath of loyalty and mutual trust, and never to reveal anything to the enemy, should we be exposed and captured even if that means torture unto death. Now, I suggest we communicate with each other in village or town names, not our villages of origin, of course. I will be known as *Zaghir*. Senai has said he will use *Afelba*. The rest of you are free to use any village of your choice.
	[The three chose Amadir, Barentu and Hagaz, respectively.]

ZAGHIR	Any question before I ask Senai to address us on the plan of action?
BARENTU	Why did we choose to meet in this place? It gives me the shivers.
AFELBA	Okay. Well, in some parts of the world, people sleep in cemeteries because they have no place to sleep. Have you seen the cemeteries in Cairo? *[It is a rhetorical question, and he continues].* Thousands sleep in cemeteries. And in parts of Palestine, children play in cemeteries for lack of fields. But that is by the way. The choice of this place is both for practical as well as for symbolic reasons. From the practical, security point of view, this is the last place where the regime's spies will think of for eavesdropping or spying in general. During the liberation struggle, we used to meet and sleep here. But more importantly, perhaps, is the symbolic reason. We need to be in communion with our martyrs.

[They all look up to him with respect and wait eagerly for him to set forth the strategy of their venture. He gives a detailed account of how the new movement of rectification and renewal began. It had been in the offing for some time, before the shameful Resolution of the Semblia, of which only he and Zhagir are members.] |
ZAGHIR	I think everything is understood. The five of us comprise the central cell. Each one of us will lead another five members of a cell. Only the leader of that cell knows his contact in the higher cell. The others only know him. And only the leader of our central cell, that is you Afelba, will know the contacts from all the other cells. The rest of us will know only the contact from our respective cell. Is this a fair summary?
AFELBA	Yes, it is. But I want to stress one thing. We have to be very careful and thorough in checking the background and trustworthiness of the people we recruit for membership of the other cells. In case of any suspicion, the central cell must be notified immediately and all activities interrupted until further notice. Are there any other questions or suggestions.
ALL FOUR	No.
AFELBA	In that case, our meeting today is over and we will meet in accordance with our agreed plan. No use of the telephone, and nothing in writing. Everything will be by word of mouth.

[They bow their heads for one minute and Afelba bids them goodnight shaking their hands one by one.]

AFELBA
We will leave as we came, one by one and through separate exits. Good night, see you in our next meeting. I will go with Zaghir because we came in one car and he is taking me back. I have an appointment to meet a friend who came from America.

Exit one by one.

SCENE TWO

[At the Café Adulis the same evening

Senai [Afelba] is chatting with two friends, customers of the Café. They are both of Senai's age, in their early fifties. Many Asmarini, of different professions and varying ages frequent Café Adulis. They come for friendly chats, to exchange gossip of the day, for social chatter, and generally for an evening relaxation. On some of the tables people are busy playing chess, while in others they are playing checkers or cards, and they keep on ordering beer or coffee or soft drinks. It is a warm and busy place and is a favorite place for government employees who eschew the government officers' club for fear of being spied upon by agents or hidden electronic gadgets.

Despite its ambience of relaxation and social intercourse, Café life has some negative aspects. To those among scholars and policy makers who are concerned with maintaining family solidarity and raising the cultural level of the urban population, the habit of spending all evenings every day at such Cafes is regrettable. Precious time that could be devoted to reading and taking evening classes and generally raising the cultural level, is wasted on idle chatter.]

SENAI
But Bandini was a good friend of his. They played golf in Rome with Bandini acting as host.

CUSTOMER WITH
THE RED CAP
Golf! That is the least of it; then you are not well informed, caro dottore. There are juicy stories that are going round, especially abroad.

THE OTHER
CUSTOMER
Such as what?

RED CAP
Hey, not so loud *[looking around their table]*. And not here. Do you want me to face the Special Court and meet the fate of Babayo and company? *[Putting his head forward and motioning the two to do the same, and whispering]*. Of course, his philandering, drinking and

lingering nightly with young ladies till the small hours of the morning is an open secret. Don't you people of the Semblia have any say at all? I mean why can't his close friends tell him to do it in secret. Or does he want to do one better than his friend Bill Clinton?

THE OTHER CUSTOMER   He has no close friend. I doubt if he ever had a close friend in his life.

RED CAP   You should know, you were in the same school. Have you ever tried to give him friendly counsel?

THE OTHER CUSTOMER   Actually, I think I have said enough. How do I know you won't misquote me in your next Internet pieces? It is all very well for you to speak, with your American passport and citizenship. If anything happens to you Uncle Sam's representative here will raise hell and have you released.

RED CAP   Come on. He won't touch you. You are one of his closest friends

THE OTHER CUSTOMER   I just told you, he knows no friend. No one was closer to him than Babayo, and you know where he is. No, I have no one to come to my rescue if I get locked up. You people living abroad do not really know the dilemma we have been facing, what we have been going through. You write your articles, you do your research and publish beautiful pieces and probably get paid for it. We have to struggle to make ends meet. *[He turns to Senai for support or confirmation, but he does not get it!].*

RED CAP   *[Exhibits a sign of disbelief].*

THE OTHER CUSTOMER   You don't believe me? Okay. Look, I was a fighter and have paid my dues in more ways than one. But I am now a middle-aged man and father of three. I can't afford to be as I used to be. Why do you think the Semblia members go along with what the Chief proposes? They are stuck here; and have no way out, and no alternative source of income. Almost all of them have children to feed and clothe. Do you think Senai, here, who is well known for his courage and dedication, would think twice if he had an alternative, except the one in the hands of the Chief? Tell him Senai, why don't you?

SENAI	What can I say? You have said it all. We have no alternative and we have families.
	[That is the most Senai can say. You can't be too careful, he thinks].
RED CAP	But your children are grown, Senai, and they can help their parents if necessary.
SENAI	What about their education? Are yours not studying in the University in New York?
RED CAP	Would you have decided to move your family abroad if you had the chance.
SENAI	Yes, I suppose I would.
RED CAP	I don't think so; you are a true believer, Senai and I know you. What about the rest of you?
OTHER CUSTOMER	We are governed by fear. Fear is the governing principle. It is the biggest part in all the present mess. Fear that something will happen: your family whenever you dare to think dangerous thoughts. Before the thoughts become action you are paralyzed by fear. And so life goes on as it is. I never felt this kind of fear when I was a fighter, before I had a family. Do you follow me?
	Red Cap is torn between an ardent desire to advance the cause for which he was sent from abroad and seek their support, on the one hand, and a growing fear that he may be betrayed by the Other Customer on the other.
SENAI	*[Equivocating with eyes fixed on the other customer]* Well, you just bear in mind the common cause of defense of our nation, and so we ask you guys to be a little more patient, that's all. And continue to be cash cows.
RED CAP	For how long, until the cows come home? *[laugher].* Until he takes this country to the dogs? Until we become another Congo or Rwanda?
SENAI	*[With his eyes fixed on the other customer whom he likes but does not trust completely these days.]* Well, just remember that we all feel the pain and are trying our best to improve things. Give us time and meanwhile, continue in your critical support.
THE CASHIER	*[Calling loudly over the din of the coffee bar]* Doctor Senai, a telephone call for you.
SENAI	Who is it?
CASHIER	He didn't say.

SENAI	Well, ask him.
CASHIER	Who is calling, please?…Dr. Senai wants to know who is calling…Okay, I'll tell him…It is your son, Yikalo, dottore.
SENAI	*[Comes towards the cashiers' desk and takes the receiver]* Yes?… …What!…Where?…What happened? I'll be there right away. *[To the cashier]* May I use your phone?
CASHIER	Yes, of course.
	[Senai dials a number and waits. There is no answer from the other side and so he goes back to the table where his two friends are waiting anxiously.]
SENAI	Sorry, I have to go. That was my son.
RED CAP	Trouble?
SENAI	Yes, I am afraid so.
RED CAP	How did he know you were here? Can I go with you?
SENAI	My family knows this is my favorite hangout. And yes Kifle, you can come if you wish.
KIFLE	*[Rising and extending his hand to the other customer]* Well, I hate to interrupt our interesting conversation. Perhaps we can resume it soon. Anyway, I am very pleased to have met you.
SENAI	*[Shaking Girmai's hand]* Sorry Girmai, but I must go. I'll see you in the office tomorrow.
GIRMAI	Anything I can do?
SENAI	No, at least not now. I really don't know. I'll tell you tomorrow.
	[Exit Senai followed by Kifle. Girmai says he'll pay for the coffee and walks slowly towards the cashier].
GIRMAI	Was that really his son on the phone?
CASHIER	Of course. Why would I say so if it were not his son?
GIRMAI	Who knows? *[Chuckling and getting closer to her and almost whispering]* Who knows the ways of romance? You bitch, you think I don't know? I have followed your footsteps and know everything about your goings and comings. I have eyes and ears everywhere. And I can expose you. Think of what your husband will do then. Think about that.

CASHIER	You can do what you damn well please. You don't impress me with your government position and your spies. You are jealous because you tried to make me your mistress and I turned you down with contempt. You are not half the man Dr. Senai is.
GIRMAI	We'll see who is man enough when your husband knows all about it.
CASHIER	*[Laughing sarcastically]* I am trembling! By the way, you go ahead and tell lies about me. I also I know a thing or two about you. And I have friends in high places.
GIRMAI	Like who?
CASHIER	Let's say he is much higher than you and more influential.
GIRMAI	*[Clenching his fists and with a murderous gaze]* You Goddam bitch!
	[Exit Girmai]

SCENE THREE

[The same evening after 8 pm. At the waiting room of a hospital ward

Senai and Kifle had left the Café Adulis and come to a private hospital to find Aster and Yikalo sitting on the sofa of the waiting room in the emergency ward.

They are all waiting quietly. Senai is chain- smoking. Kifle looks at him from time to time and waits for Senai to speak. Failing in that, and being an impatient soul and finding the silence oppressive, he addresses Aster.]

KIFLE	What did the doctors say is the prognosis?
ASTER	They said she will pull through, but the healing will take a long time.
KIFLE	Thank Goodness. And the police? Yikalo, what are the police doing?
YIKALO	They took his body to the morgue for autopsy and said they will wait till Askalu is fully conscious and able to speak before they question her.
SENAI	Well, there is nothing that we can do. We may as well go home.
ASTER	You go on, I'll stay here overnight.
KIFLE	You can come back early in the morning. There is nothing you can do; the nurses will take care of her.

ASTER	I know, but I will not be able to sleep at home, thinking of her here. You go on ahead. You can stay in our house and keep Senai company.
KIFLE	Okay, then. Let's go. *[Turning to Senai]* Come on buddy, let's go. Yikalo, let's go.
	[Exit, Senai, Kifle and Yikalo … Enter a nurse and an elderly nun who is also in charge of the many nurses of the hospital.]
NURSE	Woizero Aster, why didn't you go home with your husband and son? We just met them outside. And they told us you decided to stay overnight. There is no need for that you know. We can take care of your daughter.
ASTER	I know you can, but I will stay jus this time, if you don't mind.
NURSE	As you wish. Well, let me find you something comfortable to sleep on.
ASTER	Thank you. I would like to pray in your hospital chapel, if I may.
NUN	The chapel is right here, round the corner.
	[They walk a few steps and enter the chapel]
THE NUN	*[Whispering]*　　I'll leave you now. If there is anything you need, anything at all, please come to me. the nurse will show you my office
ASTER	*[Managing a smile in spite of the venue and the solemnity of the occasion, and shakes the nun's hand warmly, because she notices the Irish brogue in the nun's speech, reminding her of the Irish nurse who was her favorite teacher at school]* Thanks, Sister, I will.
NUN	Bless you my child, and don't worry, Askalu will pull through. We will all pray for her.
ASTER	You already know her name.
NUN	Of course, I do. She comes to Mass every Sunday, and she told me about her story and yours.
	[Exit nun, leaving Aster face to face with a large statue of the Holy Virgin standing on one corner of the chapel. The scene is so affecting and familiar that she feels a shiver down her spine and she is transported to her childhood. She makes a sign of the cross and kneels before the statue of he Holy Virgin.]

ASTER	*[Her tears streaming down her cheeks]* Hail Mary, full of Grace. The Lord is with Thee. Blessed Art Thou among women, and Blessed Is the Fruit of Thy womb, Jesus. Holy Mary, Mother of God, Pray for us sinners, now and at the hour of our death... Have pity on me in this my hour of darkness. Help me save my daughter. I ask...I ask...
	[She breaks down and lets out a long, agonized cry of despair, falling prostrate at the foot of the statue...The chapel door opens slowly and the Irish nun comes in and kneels beside Aster and weeps with her. She enfolds Aster in her arms and they stay in this position for a short while. Then the nun gets up and pulls Aster from the floor].
NUN	Come dear child. The Lord will hear your cry. Our Lady of Mercy will intercede on your behalf. I tell you it will happen; you mark my words.
ASTER	I believe you sister, and thank you.
NUN	Don't thank me, thank Him *[pointing to the picture of the crucified Christ].*
	He is the one who will work the miracle for you and your daughter. Do you believe me now?
ASTER	Oh, I do. I do.
	[As they get out of the building and walk towards the nuns' headquarters, they hear noises of people speaking loudly, arguing. They seem to be speaking at the same time and at cross-purpose. One female voice is heard loud and clear and at least two male voices. Aster, recognizing the female voice, tells the nun the visitors are her people. They walk towards the gate where the row is taking place.]
ASTER	Saba!
NUN	It is okay, guard, these people have special permission to enter.
	[Guard opens the gate and Saba and Yonas enter. Saba and Aster embrace and start crying on each other's shoulders.]
SABA	I just heard the news. How is she? Where is she?
ASTER	The doctors think she will survive, but they are not certain. She had surgery and is in the recovery room, under heavy sedation.

SABA	Can I see her?
ASTER	I am afraid not, no one is allowed for some time.
SABA	How long is sometime?
NURSE	Nobody can tell. The doctor gave me strict orders, no one is to be allowed in.
NUN	She will be alright. The Lord will take care of her. Come my dears.

[She leads them to the nuns' headquarters where the aroma of food being cooked coming from the kitchen fills the air. The scene brings back childhood memories. She remembers that during lent she was required to make certain sacrifices such as not eating some of her favorite things like chocolate, and the vestry full of purple vestments. The elderly nun goes into the kitchen to supervise the preparation of the meal, leaving the three.]

YONAS	Woizero Aster, we came as soon as we heard. What really happened?
ASTER	We don't know much except that the killer had been tailing her for some time. She noticed him following her, a couple of times and she notified one of the youth leaders about it. The police talked to that person and all we know comes from his statement. The police have not finished their investigation. They are hoping that Askalu can give them more information when she wakes up. *[She looks down and adds]* If she ever wakes up. That's all we know.
NUN	She will wake up.
ASTER	I hope you are right.
YONAS	Who is he?
ASTER	It seems he was a member of the Students and Youth Association, and he followed her to one of their meetings. Apparently, he went to the meeting and at the conclusion of the meeting he left the meeting room ahead and waited for her to come out. What actually went on between the two of them to cause him to try to kill her is not known.
YONAS	*[Morose and remorseful]* Oh my God! I think I know who it is. It is Hadgu. He did tell me that he likes to watch her walking to the youth meetings. Since she did not respond to his attempts to talk to her, he resorted

	to just watching her. I thought he was a regular fellow, you know a normal human being. I even told Askalu once that he is a nice person; but she had better instincts because she told me that she didn't think he was nice. I suppose it is feminine intuition.
SABA	But I thought he was nice too. It is just that Askalu was not attracted to him. And she did not agree with his politics. And she had some intuition that he was not a good man. We should have listened to her.

[Enter three nuns with trays of food, followed by the head nun. They are all smiles and apologize for being late in serving dinner. The head nun assigns seats to everybody. She says grace and they all start eating silently. The only sound is the cling clang of the crockery.

ASTER	*[Addressing the elderly nun]* Excuse me Sister, I don't even know your name.
THE ELDERLY NUN	Forgive me my dear. How careless of me. I am Sister Maria Faustina.

[She then introduces the rest of her sisters, four in all, including one that just walked in from outside. Saba notes the name of the curious nun. It is Sister Delores].

SABA	May I ask you a question Sister Maria Faustina?
EMMA	Of coure you may, the question is can I can answer it. *[She bursts into a warm infectious laughter. Everyone joins her and Saba looks embarrassed].* Go ahead, my dear, ask me.
SABA	Do you observe a vow of silence during meal? I mean, are we causing you to break your rules?
EMMA	Well, bless your little heart. The answer is, no. Quite the contrary the meal time is the occasion when we let our hairs down as the young ones say these days. Don't take me literally, mind you, we do not let our hairs down. *[Laughter].* But we do relax and tell each other our little stories, and joke and even gossip—yes gossip. So, don't worry, my dear. And now may I ask *you* a personal question?
SABA	Yes, of course.
EMMA	Have you any plans to get married to this handsome young man?
SABA	*[Somewhat embarrassed]* That is a question you should perhaps address to the handsome young man.

EMMA	I have no doubt but that he would want to marry you, if you'll have him. He would be a fool not to marry a beautiful girl like you. Isn't that right, Sister Delores?
SISTER DELORES	I agree, Mother Superior. *[Sister Delores giggles and turns to Saba]*.
EMMA	Sister Delores always giggles, even when she has a tooth ache. It is a special gift; I wish I had it. *[Turning to Aster]* Woizero Aster, you have hardly touched your dinner. You have to eat my dear and leave the rest to the Lord. Stop worrying and think positive, my dear.
ASTER	I have eaten enough, thank you, Sister Maria Faustina.
YONAS	*[Noticing Aster's sad face and wishing to steer the conversation to the previous topic]* Sister Faustina, I assure you that I do indeed intend to marry Saba, if she'd have me. My parents approve and I am hoping that hers will approve. I don't believe in the traditional practice of dowries, so I don't expect dowries from her parents. But I do follow our tradition of sending an elder as intermediary to the parents of the future bride. But if I may change the subject, may I ask you a question that borders on politics?
EMMA	We are not allowed to meddle in politics. But I will hear the question and let you know if I can answer it.
YONAS	Although you are a religious order, you travel with your nation's passport and the envoy of your nation is required to protect your rights in case of need. Am I right? *[Maria Faustina nods gravely]*. Well, recently the envoy of your group of European nations was expelled because he requested our government to heed international standards of human rights.
EMMA	Yes, that is right. I have an Irish passport and the Italian ambassador to this country speaks for Ireland as a member of the European Union. So far, I am not meddling in politics, I don't think *[Laughter]*.
YONAS	No you are not. Now do you think he was right in reminding our government of their obligations to observe international human rights principles and standards?
EMMA	Help me sisters. Was he right?

[As the mother superior, she is not supposed to ask for help from her junior sisters. But Maria Faustina

is nothing if not discreet, even though passion lurks in her old heart. And she did not want to give the impression that she, or her Order, is not concerned with human rights issues in the country where she serves. Her understanding of Christian charity includes deep concern for the rights of fellow human beings wherever they may be. Three nuns, all Europeans, turned to Sister Delores who answered the call].

SISTER DELORES   If I may, Mother Superior, I think the ambassador was right and that our government was wrong in expelling him.

EMMA   Sister Delores who, as you can see, is no European, but shares my values, was educated at Dublin University and holds a Masterate in European History. Does that answer your question?

YONAS   Yes it does, but it is only her views. What do you think the Vatican will say if asked the same question? I am not Catholic, but Saba is, and I have to tread carefully, here. *[Laughter].* But a historic institution that cares for the souls of human beings should surely be actively engaged in the promotion and protection of human rights. I don't see that happening. Where is the cry of anguish that Christ would expect from his Vicar and his agents everywhere when human beings are being crushed by tyrants all over the world? *[Saba kicks Yonas' leg under the table and he stops instantly to everybody's surprise].* Sorry, I got carried away; I am a Protestant Minister's son and can't help it sometimes.

EMMA   That is quite alright, my dear. I don't blame you. I used to be a human rights activist myself in South America and was expelled from there by an oppressive government which has since been overthrown, thank God. But on one thing I disagree with you. Have you heard of liberation theology? *[Yonas shakes his head].* It was before your times. Many clergymen stood on the side of the oppressed in Latin America and some paid with their lives. I still feel the passion of those days when we used to agitate for change, and I wish these tired old bones were young for me to do what I did then all over again.

YONAS   *[Surprised and smiling at the good nun with admiration]* Thank you for correcting me on that. I wish we had more men and women of God like that nowadays.

EMMA	Perhaps you will. Each period in history has it heroes and saints. And each situation begets it own solution. Be patient, vigilant and brave. And now I think we have said enough and it is bedtime.

[They all scramble to their feet, thank the nuns for the meal and file out of the room. Sister Delores gets out to see them to the door. While walking towards the gate she tells Saba that she knows her from childhood but that Saba does not know her. Saba is puzzled and asks how and where did the young nun know her. She is answered with a mysterious smile and equally mysterious words]. |
| SISTER DELORES | One of these days, I'll tell you. And I will be at your wedding, cooking. *[Giggles]*. And Yonas, I agree with you one hundred percent about what you said regarding what Christian charity should involve. I will talk to you soon. Good night and God bless you all. |

SCENE FOUR

[Two weeks later, at the home of Dr. Senai and Aster

It is Sunday in the early afternoon. The living room and the dining room are filled with people—relatives and friends who have come to commiserate with the family on the tragic happening concerning their daughter. The relatives consisting of Aster's elder sister and her husband, who live in the country side, Senai's younger brother and his wife and an old uncle of his, are huddled round the dinning table and conversing quietly. Aster is explaining to the rest what she knew about what happened to the relatives who listen in puzzlement and concern. Those in the dining room are mostly Senai's friends and co-workers at the Ministry of Local Government— six persons in all and all male. Three people are doing most of the talking—Kifle who has his red cap on, and the two known as Zagir and Hagaz.]

KIFLE	*[Addressing Hagaz]*Yes, but consider this. What if the Arabs, once they have their state, start to subvert the state of Israel? I hate Sharon as much as any one. I will never forget what he did in Sabra and Shatila in 1982. In fact, in my view he should face the Hague Tribunal for crimes against humanity. But why do you think he was elected last year after the uprising? Because, ordinary Israeli feel insecure and he plays on that sense of insecurity. Now I, a neutral observer, find it hard to blame the Israelis for fearing the Arabs.

HAGAZ	Why would the Arabs want to subvert Israel? They have their own problems of daily existence, of poverty and irresponsible governments. So, why do you think the Arabs, or the Palestinians to be exact, wish Israelis any harm when they have their own daily problems to think about?
KIFLE	Well, to begin with, it is not the ordinary Arabs that I am thinking about. It is the fanatics ands politicians.
HAGAZ	The politicians can actually gain much by cooperation with Israel with its dynamic society and economy.
KIFLE	And the fanatics, Hamas and the Bin Ladens?
HAGAZ	Keep Bin Laden out of this; he was only using the Palestinian issue for his own evil goal.
KIFLE	They all used the Palestinian issue for their own goals, beginning with Egypt's Gamal Abdel Nasser. They kept the issue alive for decades by maintaining a permanent Palestinian refugee population.
ZAGIR	These refugees were expelled from their homes, their ancestral homes by the government of the newly created Israel in 1948. They were expelled en mass and their homes and farms taken over by the Jews. And the United Nations recognizes them as refugees and their right of return to their ancient homeland. It isn't as if they were interlopers who trespassed on somebody else's property. Their land was stolen from them. Now what makes the Jews' right of claim to those lands better than those of the Arabs whose ancestors had settled on them. And Arabs and Jew had lived in peace and harmony for centuries until the European Jews came with their Zionist ideology, to escape persecution. I fee great sympathy for the victims of persecution, but it seems to me that the former victims of persecution are now engaged in victimizing others.
	[Hagaz has become emotional and sweating. Senai notices this, having known him for years as his comrade-in-arms in the trenches. Senai decides it is time to steer the conversation away from this controversial subject before Zaghir explodes and spoil the afternoon.]
SENAI	Well even those who won Nobel Prize for peace have not solved this difficult problem. We cannot solve it here; perhaps we should change the subject and try to solve the problem of the price of eggs in China. *[They all laugh]*.

ZAGIR	Or the price of eggs in Asmara. Charity begins at home.
KIFLE	Since I brought the subject of Arab-Israeli conflict, I am to blame for any misunderstanding.
	[He turns toward Hagaz who, still sweating, looks menacingly at Kifle. And again Senai, wishing to avoid a fallout between his friends who do not know each other tries another tactic.]
SENAI	No, I was the one who brought the subject after we heard the radio news about the deteriorating situation there. So, if there is to be any responsibility, I am responsible. But it is natural for us to talk about current issues of interest, and it is also natural and healthy to have different points of view. And, yes, charity should begin at home. We are all feeling the effects of a rising cost of living. The question is what is being done about it.
HAGAZ	Does our friend from America understand this problem, I wonder?
KIFLE	*[Annoyed]* I understand it more than you think. I, too, have relatives who live and suffer like the rest of you, you know.
SENAI	Kifle is raising seven siblings and nephews paying for their education and helping their parents. In short, he is giving back from there what he didn't take from here. *[He emphasizes the word "here" and "there" and watched Hagaz's reaction].*
KIFLE	You don't have to say that Senai; it sounds like I was bragging when I told you about my relatives. I spoke to you about it when you ad I were talking about duties owed by citizens living abroad. What they are paying to the government like the two percent of their incomes and all the rest of it. It is my own way of giving back to society. One of the small ways anyhow. I am sure others do it in different ways. Anyway, it is nothing to brag about. So you don't have to keep praising me for doing my duty.
SENAI	Ah, but I do, because it is rare. You are one of a kind my dear friend. I wish one tenth of our people out there were like you.
HAGAZ	*[Contrite and utterly moved by the exchange between Senai and Kifle]*
	I am sorry if I seemed rude. It isn't every day that one meets people like you who do not forget their relatives.

I wish my brothers in America were like you. Again, I am sorry.

KIFLE   [*Extending a hand and shaking Hagaz'z hand*] No offence taken, and no apology needed. Besides, I do share some of your views. In a way, I was just being the devil's advocate.

HAGAZ   So then, you are on the side of the angels. [*Laughter and general relaxation*].

KIFLE   I hope so. I am definitely on the side of the angels here, in our country. I am one of the lucky devils who escaped and made some money in New York. I tried to bring much of that money here in the form of investments. But there is not much encouragement here. Too many obstacles. Too much resentment of those of us who made it abroad. You guys who gave your youth to liberate the land from alien occupation have to let those of us who chickened out then to pay our dues now in a different way. We love you, we respect and honor you. But you also need to respect our offer of help. Instead of resenting us, try to use us for the common cause. When are you going to change this division into "Them and Us", this Tegedalai versus Gebar? It is offensive and is not helpful to the country. This has to change.

SENAI   I think you have made your case very well, Kifle. As they used to say in NewYork, "cool it baby, the message has been delivered." That was after they cried, "burn baby, burn." Remember? [*Kifle nods with a smile and Senai rises to go to the kitchen*]. I am going to have more coffee. More coffee anyone?

[*Senai returns with Aster who is carrying a tray with small plates filled with barley Qolo to the men's delight. She then signals Senai to follow her to the kitchen to which they both disappear*].

ASTER   I am going to the hospital with the rest of the relatives. You can join us after the guests leave. But don't rush them. By the way, we could hear the argument. Some voices were raised. What was that all about?

SENAI   Nothing; it was the usual banter and some sensitive nerves were touched. But it ended peacefully.

ASTER   Some one was getting at Kifle, I could hear that much. I wish people would accept the fact that some Eritreans are luckier or smarter, or both, and did well to leave home and go abroad as refugees instead of chasing the mirage we called liberation struggle.

SENAI	Aster, you can't mean that!
ASTER	Yes, I do. Look where it has got us. We gave our lives, our professions to the so-called cause of liberation. And look where we are. Confused, helpless in the face of brute force and lawlessness. What have the police done to investigate the case of Askalu's attempted murder? We have talked to them a hundred times, and all they tell us is to wait. And your friends in the Party and government can't even help. They are probably enjoying our predicament. And the doctors at the hospital are pitiful. They change their minds on Askalu's prognosis from day to day. And the hospital is a mess. We had far better service in Sahel.
SENAI	You are upset and I am equally angry at everything. But to say they are enjoying our predicament is stretching it too far. By the way, Kifle is insisting that we should send her to America as soon as possible. He is convinced that she will not be helped given the poor hospital facilities here. And I agree with him, about sending her to America, I mean. He is willing to take her himself. He has called his friends in New York to make the arrangements. What do you think?
ASTER	Then I will go with her and stay with her a few days and come back.
SENAI	Fine. Yikalo and I will manage. But we'll miss you both.

[Aster leaves with the rest of their relatives. As she reaches the gate she sees Sister Delores parking her Volkswagon beetle. After she parks the car, Saba and Yonas emerge and wave to Aster. She tells her relatives to go to the hospital ahead of her and she will join them soon. She greets the three new visitors and asks them to come in.]

ASTER	Sister Delores, what a nice surprise, and how did you meet these two?
SISTER DELORES	I have been meaning to come to visit you ever since we had dinner together last time, but I have been out of town to the Keren area on Mission work. How are you
ASTER	I am alright and you?
SISTER DELORES	Fine. We have a surprising piece of news.
SABA	Yes, I couldn't wait to tell you.
ASTER	What is it?

SABA	You will never believe this but Sister Delores whose real name was Ghenet is actually my sister.
ASTER	What!
SABA	Yes. Isn't it wonderful? I have lived as an only child and always wished I could have a sister. That is one reason why I became close to Askalu. I consider her like my sister, as you know. And now I have another sister, and elder sister this time.
ASTER	Well what happened, I mean how did it happen? What am I saying? I am confused. Come in and tell me all about it.
SABA	Well, it seems that my late father, who died when I was only ten, had an affair as a young man and impregnated Sister Delores' mother and then disappeared when her mother's relatives were looking to get him. He went to Ethiopia and married my mother in Addis Ababa. What a society we had!
	[They go into the house as the rest of the guests were filing out one by one, thanking Aster for the hospitality and expressed their hopes that Askalu will survive. The new guests are seated in the lounge and offered coffee and cakes which they begin to consume quietly until Senai settles down on one of the sofas opposite Yonas].
YONAS	Where is Yikalo?
SENAI	He is running some errands for me. He will come later.
SABA	Dr. Senai, I want to introduce my sister. *[She points to Sister Delores].*
SENAI	What do you mean? She is a nun and, therefore, everyone's sister.
SABA	No, she is my real sister.
SENAI	Really? Where have you been hiding her? *[Turning to Sister Delores]* I am happy to meet you, Sister.
SISTER DELORES	My great pleasure to meet you at last, Dr. Senai. I have known about you for many years, even before liberation.
SABA	You are full of surprises. How did you come to know about him?
SISTER DELORES	There are many things I haven't told you about me, and my past. I will soon.
SENAI	I wonder, were you involved in our struggle for independence at some stage by any chance? *[Sister*

	Delores answers with a non-committal and intriguing smile that neither denies nor affirms Senai's question. So, he decides not to press her, but so intrigued was he by her that he was determined to meet her and says so. For now, he was curious to find out more about what she does in her present work]. What does your Mission do and how long has it been in operation here?
SISTER DELORES	Our Mission does charity work which sometimes includes sheltering and educating abandoned children and orphans. The Mission is called Sisters of Divine Mercy, and it is new here.
SENAI	Is that a new Order?
SISTER DELORES	No, it has been in existence for some time. The Mother Superior is an old member of the Order and we persuaded her to come and open a Mission here which she did a couple of years ago. I came with her and have been here from the beginning. Any more probing questions? *[She giggles surprising Aster].*
SENAI	You may think I am prying too much into your private domain? I have been curious to know the work of religious Non-Governmental Organizations [NGOs] in part because it falls in my official function. But partly also out of an enduring intellectual interest. I mean where does religious duty of human charity end and politics begin or vice versa. Am I making sense?
SISTER DELORES	You can ask any question you want, Dr. Senai; I was being facicious and naughty. It is my nature. And now, may I ask you a personal question?
SENAI	Go ahead.
SISTER DELORES	Did you take part in the decision of the National Assembly, which charged the veteran fighters with treason?
SENAI	*[Embarrassment showing on his face]* I am afraid so.
SISTER DELORES	At the time it happened, we were arguing with some friends and I was holding the ground in your favor, arguing that you were not involved in that shameful decision. It seems I was wrong and the others were right.
SENAI	Well, I stand humbled before you, guilty as charged, guilty of the "shameful decision," as you call it.
SISTER DELORES	*[Scrutinizing his face to see whether he was really contrite or simply mocking her]* As you know, I am in the business of saving tortured souls. Redemption

is always possible for those who are truly remorseful. *[Rising from her seat]* Are you remorseful Dr. Senai, I mean truly remorseful?

SENAI   *[Taken completely by surprise and looking around him only to be greeted by two pairs of inquisitive eyes, he rises to face Sister Delores]* Of course I am remorseful. I am ashamed more than you can imagine. I can only say, in my defense, that I did try to challenge the process of accusing people of such heinous crimes without due process. I know it is not enough to say this in view of the seriousness of the harm we did.

ASTER   He has not had a peace of mind since then; I am a witness.

SISTER DELORES   Please, forgive me; I did not mean to add more pain to what must be a very painful experience for you. It is just that you occupy a special place in many people's hearts as a true *tegadalai* and decent human being. And what your National Assembly did on February 2, is contrary to decency and unworthy of a true *tegadalai*, that's all. I just couldn't contain myself; excuse me.

SENAI   Please, don't apologize, you are right in everything you said. But you are indeed full of surprises. I never expected a young nun to be so passionately engaged in politics.

SISTER DELORES   What happened on February 2 goes beyond politics. It defies all morality. It is against common sense and an insult to the nation as a whole. And don't forget, even as a nun, I am a member of this nation, for good or for ill. When I have the chance, I would like to share with you some ideas about improving the conditions of our people as well as other issues.

SENAI   I would welcome that. Any time.

SISTER DELORES   Okay. Well, I must go now.

SENAI   No, you must stay longer. Aster, is there more coffee?

SISTER DELORES   Sorry, I must go. Duty calls. Saba, let's go, or do you want to stay longer?

SABA   No, I will go with you and I'll join Aster at the hospital.

[Exit Sister Delores and Saba, leaving Senai and Aster sitting in silence. Senai breaks the silence].

SENAI   Interesting person, don't you think?

ASTER	Intriguing more than interesting. *[More silence]*. Are you sure you don't know her?
SENAI	What is that supposed to mean? Of course I am sure I don't know her. *[More silence, again broken by Senai]*. Come on Aster, what did you mean by that? What did you have in mind?
ASTER	Well, it is her entire behavior as well as what she said about you. Those were not the words of a nun. Is she really a nun? And I repeat did you know her before?
SENAI	And I repeat, I did not know her. I never set eyes on her before today. And you are being irrational. By the way, weren't you going to the hospital?
ASTER	That's right, get rid of me, and push the problem under the rug. But the problem will not disappear.
SENAI	My God, Aster, are you crazy?
ASTER	Yes I am crazy. I am crazy with helplessness. My daughter is lying in hospital half alive; I don't know if she will live or die. And my husband is philandering, and there is nothing I can do about it.
SENAI	You are really out of your mind. Askalu's fate is as much a source of pain for me as it is for you, and her condition is as frustrating for me as it is for you. As for your wild accusation of philandering, I don't think I need to answer it. If you believe it there is nothing I can do about it.
ASTER	Do you deny that you have been having an affair with the cashier in the Caffe Adulis?
SENAI	*[Thunderstruck, and for the first time, at a loss for words]* Where did you get such a wild idea?
ASTER	*[Producing a piece of paper]* This is the source of the wild idea. Have fun reading it, Now I will go to the hospital.
SENAI	No, wait. I will explain. *[Continues to read the piece of type-written note]*. This note is partly true, but it is dead wrong and malicious on the accusation that I have a child by this woman. And I have an idea who wrote it. *[He sits down beside her and tries to take her hand which she withdraws]*.
ASTER	Don't touch me.
SENAI	Aster, I have been living with guilt ever since I had this brief affair. I feel a profound regret and I owe you an

	explanation. But the child is not mine. She can confirm this if you want to meet her.
ASTER	Okay let's go and confront the bitch.
SENAI	If you meet her, talk to her and hear her story, you wouldn't say that she is a bitch. She is a very nice woman who happens to have a bad husband. I am not trying to defend what I did. I am not proud of what I did, but it was a very brief encounter which came out of a meeting in my office
ASTER	What was she doing in your office?
SENAI	She came to talk to me in confidence about her domestic problems. Her husband who is one of the people who work with me at the office was spending his salary gambling and drinking and was not giving her any money. She didn't have a job at the time and she and her two young boys were facing starvation. Some one advised her to talk to me to help her find a solution.
ASTER	She has three children not two, and one of them is yours.
SENAI	You haven't heard a word I said. The third child was born after he got the job and had mended his ways.
ASTER	He was abroad studying over a year and that is when she had the baby. That is what the note says.
SENAI	Yes, that is what it says because it was written by the man who impregnated her.
	[Losing his temper]. I see that nothing I say will convince you. Well, there is only one way out of this. We will both go to the Café Adulis and we will have this out with her and be done with it once and for all. I have been living with the shadow of guilt hanging over my head like the sword of Democles.
ASTER	Alright, let us go and have it out with her.
	[They walk into their Toyota Corolla and drive all the way to the Cafe Adulis in silence].

50

SCENE FIVE

[Later on the same day at the office of the manager of the Café Adulis

Senai has arranged with the manager of the Café Adulis who is an old school friend, to make his office available for a delicate private meeting in which the cashier is involved. The manager volunteered to hold the fort at the cash register for the duration of the meeting. Senai made the perfunctory introduction and the two women nodded at each other nervously and sat down round a small table opposite each other with Senai taking the chair, so to speak.]

SENAI *[Addressing the cashier]* Almaz, we have come to talk to you about the short affair you and I had. Aster received a note from an unknown person claiming that you and I have been having the affair for a long time, that we are still having the affair and that your third son is mine. *[Almaz shows great surprise]*

ALMAZ That son of a dog! I know who is spreading this. It must be he who wrote that note.

ASTER Are you saying you never had an affair with my husband?

  [Almaz turns to Senai for guidance]

SENAI You can tell her the truth Almaz, the whole truth.

ALMAZ Excuse me Woizero Aster, but you have it all wrong. Yes we did have an affair, which lasted for about a month, not even that. I would be a liar if said that I did not fall for your husband. I fell in love with him and was heart-broken when he told me he could not continue with the affair. He told me he loved and respected you too much to continue. He was very kind and helped me through the most difficult time of my marriage. And I am eternally grateful to him. He may not know it, but he has some enemies who are close to him. They appear as friends but are really his enemies. I can name names if you want. I have no doubt as to who wrote that note.

SENAI Who do you think wrote it?

ALMAZ I am sure it is your friend Girmai.

SENAI Girmai Araia from my office?

ALMAZ I have good reason for thinking it is him.

  [Almaz recounts the incident in the Café Adulis in which Girmai threatened to reveal her affair as well as other incidents in which he tried to go out with her without success and he repeated the same threat].

ASTER	What about the paternity of your third boy? The note said that you had him during your husband's absence.
ALMAZ	That is true. I will tell you what happened and I trust that you will do me the favor of keeping it in confidence. You see woizero Aster, some of your *tegadelti*, especially those at the very top have become loose donkeys who prey on all young women they lay their eyes on and find ways of luring them to hotels and sexually assaulting them. I was a victim of such assault. The result was my third boy. When I told your friend Girmai about this, he cracked a joke and couldn't stop laughing at his own joke. Do you know what he said? He told me I was deflowered by the Dergue and Shamrocked by Shaebia. The son of a bitch!
ASTER	But what about your husband? Didn't he suspect that the baby as not his?
AMAZ	Of course he did. But when I told him who the father was he kept quiet. So much for our heroic manhood! This did not happen even during the Dergue's rule.
SENAI	Any other question, Aster?
ASTER	No, I have my answers and thank you, Almaz. I wish you and your children all the best.
ALMAZ	And I wish you al the best. I was so sorry to hear about your daughter.
ASTER	[Rising] Goodbye.
ALMAZ	Goodbye woizero Aster. Good by Dr. SENAI. I wish you all the best.

[Almaz goes to take up her post at the cash register, and Senai stops to thank the manager. Then he takes Aster by the arm and shepherds her out of the Café, which was already filled with customers. Senai and Aster walk towards their car. She tells him to drop her at the hospital. He decides to go with her to the hospital].

ACT THREE

Anatomy of Political Terror

SCENE ONE

[At the Interrogation Center of the Special Security.]

TEKLU

*[The fearsome head of the dreaded Halewa TseTita (Special Security is getting his desk ready for the day's) business. That business is interrogation of witnesses who are to testify in the pending secret trial of "foreign agents," "defeatists" and "enemies **of the people**." Some of these, who were detained en masse on the order of the Boss aka the Almighty one, were Teklu's comrades-in-arm and of the Boss during the fight for freedom. They fought for the country's freedom but are now robbed of it themselves!]*

TEKLU

[Ignoring his ingratiating subordinate, continues taking notes from a file... Suddenly and peremptorily] go and bring me my cigarettes.

[Enter PW1 in handcuffs, accompanied by two grim-looking security guards. PW1 is a man in his late thirties with receding, grizzled hair and a pair of sharp eyes that dart left and right with timorous curiosity. Obviously, he has not been faring well recently as evidenced by his sad countenance, sunken cheeks and emaciated body. Still there is some dignity left in him, surviving weeks of mental and physical torture. That irreducible minimum of pride, with a touch of reverse contempt, that even the

lowly among us feel is visible in the way PW1 looks at his tormentors now that he has got a breathing space. How long it will last he does not know, as they play cat-and-mouse game with him.]

TEKLU *[Smiling to PW1 and pointing to one of the chairs]* Sit down, sit down, please. *[Turning to one of the security guard]* And take off his handcuffs. This is a civilized country. When are you, people going to be civilized, for Heaven's sake? Haven't you heard about the Geneva Conventions?

[As PW1 bows his head while one of the men removes his handcuffs, Teklu steals a wink at the standing guard who looked confused by Teklu's strange questions.]

TEKLU Bring him tea and a couple of panini, and then leave us.

[As the guards leave, Teklu beams at the prisoner and tries to put on his charm] You have to excuse these eager beavers. You must understand, of course, they are only doing their job. But in doing their job they sometimes overstep the boundaries of decency and human consideration. *[Unimpressed with Teklu's evident hypocrisy, PW1 continues in bowed head and silence].* How have they been treating you?

PW1 Before or after the torture?

TEKLU *[Taken aback by this unexpected pluck but putting up a brave front, he chuckles]* I see you have not lost your sarcasm. I have heard a lot about you and I have been impressed by what they reported to me. They reported that it took a very long time to break you down. You were the toughest nut to crack, and I suppose you must have become a challenge to these people who are used to getting confessions at the slightest threat of violence. But I must warn you, don't push your luck. We have infinite resources and infinite methods of persuasion. You have a family don't you? Children?

[He moves his head nearer PW1 for close observation and notices a cloud of anxiety invading the prisoner's face, a narrowing of the eyes and a furrowing of the forehead].

PW1 Why do you ask?

TEKLU Oh, just curiosity. But don't think for one moment that your ordeal is over unless you cooperate. You'd do well to concentrate on cooperating with us. Why risk more agony when there is the prospect of reward? If

	you cooperate, we can do favors for you beyond your wildest imagination.
PW1	Like what?
TEKLU	Good question. Well, are you ready for a good deal from which you will benefit, no questions asked?
PW1	I am listening? What deal are you offering me?
TEKLU	If you back up your confessions with a sworn oral testimony when you appear in court next week, we are prepared to issue you a passport under an assumed name, find you a scholarship and settle you in a country of your choice with a $10,000 starting amount, until you find a job and settle down. Ten thousand dollars which is over 150,000 Nakfa at the official rate. Can you imagine!

A knock on the door, and a young girl aged about twelve comes with a tray of two cups of tea and two loafs of bread.

| TEKLU | Put it on the table, sweetie and leave it, we will pour the tea ourselves. Tell the guard outside to come in. |
| YOUNG GIRL | *[Gazing at PW1]* Yes sir. |

[The young girl keeps gazing at PW1 with obvious interest. He notices her gaze but does not react. As she leaves, her eyes swell up which PW1 notices, but not Teklu. She leaves the room, closing the door behind her and stealing a last look at the prisoner.]

TEKLU	Drink your tea and eat the bread. This is good bread from the Party's bakery. *[He takes a piece from the bread, eats it and gives the rest to PW1]*. So what do you say?
PW1	*[Sipping the tea and munching the bread]* It sounds attractive. What guarantee do I have that you will honor your promise after I testify? *[He waits and adds]*. That is if I agree to testify.
TEKLU	You have my word of honor.

[PW1 chokes on the bread and makes a mess of the edge of the desk. He tries to clear the mess while at the same time he tries to hide his amusement. The choke brings tears to his eyes].

| TEKLU | Be careful now, don't you choke to death when you have great things ahead of you. Drink the tea and clear your throat. |

PW1	*[Recovering but still smiling]* I am alright now.
TEKLU	Did I say something funny that sent the bread to your windpipe?
PW1	Oh no.
TEKLU	I think I know why, but never mind. Where were we?
PW1	I asked you what guarantees do I have that you will not go back on your word. You said, "You have my word of honor". *[This time he was careful not to show any sign of amusement].*
TEKLU	Oh yes. By the way, it is okay to laugh. I am a man with a sense of humor. Now, if my word of honor is not sufficient collateral, then I will try another one. I mean if you choke on a mere mention of my word of honor, I won't risk losing you to a choking incident. That would be absurd wouldn't it? No, instead I will swear on the blood of our martyrs. I see from the file you were a freedom fighter, so that should mean something to you.
PW1	*[Controlling his anger with difficulty]* Yes, it does mean something to me, more than you can imagine.
TEKLU	Which was your last Unit?
PW1	Unit 72 and 09.
TEKLU	Both?
PW1	Yes, both.
TEKLU	Did you know Paulos before you became a member of his Unit?
PW1	You will find it all in the file. I did not know him personally before I became a member of his Unit, but I knew him by reputation.
TEKLU	And after liberation?
PW1	After liberation the Unit was dissolved and its members dispersed.
TEKLU	Come on, I know that. I mean did you have contacts with him after liberation.
PW1	I was with the forces in Asab and elsewhere. We met a few times whenever I came to Asmara.
TEKLU	When was the last time you met him?
PW1	During the Hannish war.
TEKLU	You can do better than that. That may be when you saw

him last, but when was the last time you really saw him? Didn't you meet him secretly in 1999 during the war with the Weyane? Now remember the $10,000 and the new life away from all this. On the other hand, think of a life of uncertain future with no chance of seeing your family. I know you have a family. You saw your daughter a few minutes ago, didn't you. You thought I didn't notice. I have eyes at the back of my head and on the sides.

[He explodes into a cruel, staccato laugher and lets it sink in PW1's mind].

PW1   Why did you use her and how did you get her here?

TEKLU   Easy. Your wife is in great need of money and we gave your daughter part-time job in our Party Cafeteria. She makes good money that helps her mother and her to survive. I am sure your wife appreciates our charity. You can ask her yourself.

PW1   Where is she?

TEKLU   Right outside. *[He rings the bell, and a uniformed guard appears].* Bring in Woizero Awetash. *[The guard salutes and leaves].* Interesting name, Awetash. Is she a Tigrean? But not a member of the Weyano, I am told. Where did you meet her? Never mind. Far be it from me to interfere in family matters. How does the Bible put it? Whom God hath united, let no man put assunder. *[Another short chuckle...]*

               [Enter Awetash. A striking woman in her early thirties, Awetash is fair in complexion with large luminous eyes and black hair cut short, Afro style. She has an altogether commanding presence and a strong face that speaks firmness of purpose and character. But she is visibly affected by the sight of the love of her life, now appearing like a shadow of his former self whom she had not seen for seven months. No sooner had she seen his emaciated face than she breaks down. Manna had stood to welcome her and rushes toward her. She wraps her arms around his neck and continues to weep, as he rocks her gently and murmurs words of endearment. Teklu watches them for a moment and walks towards the door].

TEKLU   Well, I'll leave you two for a while. I am sure you have a lot to talk about. And Manna, remember the offer I made you. I expect your answer after you two have had a family chat. I'll see you in about an hour.

[*Exit Teklu, and Manna enfolds Awetash in a rapturous embrace. They stay entwined for a while, kissing until they are almost out of breath. Panting for breath and their hearts pounding, they sit down on two chairs facing each other. He continues to hold her hands and gazes in her eyes, as she tries to wipe the tears*].

MANNA   When did they tell you I was here?

AWETASH   Last night. And today, they sent a courier to tell me to come to the security office.

MANNA   When did they employ Titi in their Cafeteria, and are you in such great need of money that you let her be employed by them?

                 [*Awetash bows her head and cries afresh. He can see that it was hard for her to accept their offer and tells her he forgives her, although it was galling for him to learn that his little Titi is working when she should concentrate on her studies*].

MANNA   How has it been?

AWETASH   Hard, very hard. The hardest part was having to beg for help. There was nobody I could depend on for help. After your arrest, most of our friends started avoiding me. Some even called me names.

MANNA   Like what?

AWETASH   Like "Lousy Agame", and "Weyane agent."

MANNA   Don't mind them. They have been brainwashed by government propaganda. When things change tomorrow, thy will rush to come to apologize. That is the way things are. Just ignore them and keep your head high. All this will pass.

AWETASH   Will it pass? When will it pass, Manna? You say when things change, but how can you say that when everything that we see and hear confirms they will be in power forever.

MANNA   Don't you believe that. It seems so on the surface, but don't be deceived by the surface. There is a lot going on underground.

AWETASH   I was so desperate at one point, I even consulted a fortune-teller in Wekidiba.

MANNA   Oh no! Why Awetash? A fortune teller! That is absurd; you of all people?

AWETASH	I know I was desperate. But I went back to the faith and sought the assistance of our Lady at the Church of Saint Mary in Asmara and even Mariam Da'Arit. I am confident you will be released. She told me so.
MANNA	Who told you so?
AWETASH	The Holy Mother. She spoke to me one foggy morning when I was in utter despair.
MANNA	Oh, please, Awetash.
AWETASH	You still don't believe, do you?
MANNA	If I am released it will not be because of the intervention of supernatural forces. If I am out of this it will be for another reason.
AWETASH	What do you mean?
MANNA	I mean they are offering me a deal to lie in court in exchange for release from prison and…[He hesitates]
AWETASH	Will that mean endangering others.
MANNA	That is the idea! I am torn between saving you and Titi from your desperate straits and staying faithful to my principles.
AWETASH	What else did they offer you?
MANNA	They promised to get me out of this country and settle me abroad.
AWETASH	I see. They want you to lie in court and put the lives of others on the line! By the way, where does that leave us?
MANNA	You are uppermost in my mind, you should know that. And I am conflicted. If I could only be sure that you will be safe and able to survive somehow, I wouldn't hesitate to tell them to go to hell. I mean I have been through the worst torture imaginable. They couldn't do to me worse things than they have already done. And I haven't promised anything. In any case, the question is, even if I decide to do as they ask how will I know that they will not go back on their words?
AWETASH	Exactly. They can turn around and send you right back to prison after your testimony causes others to die.
MANNA	Of course, the alternative could be indefinite imprisonment. What do you think.
AWETASH	Well I wont lie to you, I am tempted. I am tempted because life has been miserable. But I cannot live with my conscience knowing that we have been the cause of

	the death of other innocent people. So I will pray to our Holy Mother and rely on her to help you.
MANNA	It is agreed then, no compromise. By the way, they have been concocting stories of collusion with the Weyane government. They are trying to implicate two or three of the main opponents. They may try to invent stories about you and me, stories of Weyane connection because of your Tigrean origin.
AWETASH	*[Angrily]* I am as good an Eritrean as any one. I was born and brought up in Idaga Arbi. I voted in the Referendum for Eritrea's independence. This is my country, and no one is going to deny me my rights as a citizen. *[They kiss again]*
TEKLU	Sorry to break this touching scene, but I did say an hour. Actually I gave you an hour and a quarter. Woizero Awetash, the visit must end now, I am afraid. I am sure there will be a happy reunion soon. Am I right Manna?
	[Awetash bows to the security chief who has her husband's life in his hands and walks out reluctantly but with dignity. She walks slowly towards the door without turning back to look at Manna].
MANNA	You told me the price you will pay. You did not tell me what I am supposed to do. What exactly is it that you want me to do?
TEKLU	That is the spirit. I am glad you decided. Well, what you need to do is testify in court that you were a messenger between Paulos and the Weyane; that you delivered messages between them while the country was at war with the Weyane.
MANNA	What else?
	[Suddenly, the telephone rings on the secure line. Teklu knows where that is from but is not sure; it could also be the secretary. He picks up the telephone and says "hello," then springs to his feet as though pinched by a sharp object. He stands to attention and repeats " Yes Sir" several times before speaking].
TEKLU	We are getting very close to making a deal with him, sir...*[Listens more and says]* I have made the offer as you ordered, sir...Yes sir, he understands...*[Listens more and continues]* She was here, sir and just left. Your idea of having her here was brilliant, sir...yes sir, we will get everything signed and delivered very soon. I will come tonight to show you the signed documents.

	[He hangs the phone very carefully a if he is afraid, the voice on the other side was still listening. He looks a little preoccupied and takes his time to recover before he addresses Manna.]
TEKLU	Now where were we?
MANNA	You were telling me what I have to do in return for the enormous favor you are prepared to do me. And I asked you, what else do you need from me? You had just started when the phone rang which I take it is from he Boss. *[Teklu's expressive face registers irritation, but he continues ignoring the remark].*
TEKLU	The main thing we want from you is to testify in court in accordance with the testimony that you will sign. That statement is already prepared. Secondly, we want you to testify that you were also acting as the go-between for Paulos and Woldu, delivering messages from them to foreign embassies and from the embassies to them.
MANNA	*[For the first time feeling a strange sense of release and loudly laughing at the startled Teklu]* Do you really believe that I will stand in court and swear to tell the untruth, the whole untruth and nothing but untruth? *[Another prolonged and almost hysterical laughter].* You are asking me to commit perjury testifying against innocent people. You offer me freedom and the other incentives in exchange for sending innocent people to the firing squad. You are asking me to sell out and sell my soul. Well, the answer, my friend is definitely, absolutely, unalterably NO! Ten thousand times NO!
TEKLU	*[Although he is angry, decides to keep calm and try his last card]* Well, you disappoint me. I gave you more credit than you deserve. You just decided to send yourself and your family to damnation. Have you thought of your wife and your children, of what would happen to them?
MANNA	What the hell do you mean?
TEKLU	Do you know anything about the history of the wives of the ministers and other officials of Emperor Haile Selassie? About what happened to them when their husbands were detained by the Dergue?
MANNA	What has that to do with anything?
TEKLU	Oh, it has everything to do with everything. Some of those wives became the concubines of sergeants and corporal and even enlisted men. Imagine, those dainty ladies—many of them as beautiful as your

	wife—becoming playthings of ignorant soldiers. Their shushus! Isn't that what you call your wife?
MANNA	You bastard! *[Manna, whose frayed nerves were wearing thin as Teklu taunted him now realizes that Teklu had bugged the room and was listening to their conversation. He explodes at the mention of his wife's term of endearment in association with the Dergue' concubines, jumps from his chair and grabs Teklu by the throat. When Teklu, who is slight in build, tries to pull out his hidden revolver, Manna picks a sharp steel letter opener and strikes at Teklu's neck with maniacal force. The steel object penetrates the area of the jugular vein and Teklu lets out a strange gurgling sound. The Guards come rushing in and one of them pulls his revolver and shoots Manna five times, one bullet going right through his head. He falls dead, with blood spluttering about and gray white matter falls by the side of his splintered head.]*
ONE GUARD	Call an ambulance. Call the emergency number of the hospital, quick. We must save His Excellency's life.
	[One guard runs out to the office where there are telephones, while the other tries to stop the bleeding from Teklu's neck. Outside the office, there is general commotion. Employees of the Security Department and workers in adjoining offices who heard the shots and come rushing to the scene are craning their necks to see what is happening. The security guard tries to warn them off without success. He blocks the office door].
THE GUARD	What is the matter with you people. Now, move on go to your works. Do you think this is a wedding ceremony? Come on, move!
A SPECTATOR	Just tell us what happened. Is His Excellency alright? The shots came from his special office.
GUARD	Yes, he is okay. Now please move. Go back to your offices. Please.
	[Some begin to move slowly and reluctantly, while others shuffle a few feet and stop. The guard gives up and stands at the door, waiting for the ambulance and the medics to arrive. Meanwhile the other guard inside has managed to stop the bleeding and tries to speak to Teklu who does not respond].

SCENE TWO

[A few Days Later. A funeral at the Enda Mariam Cemetery.

Teklu is buried, with full honors, at the Martyrs Cemetery, with all the government dignitaries attending. The issue of Manna's burial place occasioned a great deal of controversy. And so, although they died the same day, Teklu was buried one day earlier as Manna's friend and relatives went back and forth to convince the powers that be to allow Manna to be buried in the Heroes Cemetery, but to no avail. As the mourners were gathering, awaiting the start of the burial ceremony, people are heard complaining.]

A MOURNER	Manna was a hero and these bastards denied him a hero's funeral.
ANOTHER MOURNER	Manna was a freedom fighter with an outstanding record. Yet he is denied this last rite. Even in death, they deny us our God-given rights. May they burn in hell!
A THIRD MOURNER	Amen! In the kingdom of the Almighty Boss, rights are defined by might, not law. *[The Officiating Pries clears his throat to begin the ceremonies.]*
OFFICIATING PRIEST	In the name of the Father, the Son and the Holy Spirit— One God, Amen. Brothers and sisters of faith, we have lost a dear brother who is departed from this earthly life. But we know, as believers that he has only died in flesh. His soul lives on and is one with the Creator. Before I pass the microphone, to a friend of the departed who is going to deliver the funeral oration, I ask all of you to bow your heads and say the Lord's prayer with me. *[He leads the mourners in saying the Lord's Prayer]*
SENAI	*[After the officiating priest tells the grieving women to stop weeping]*

Dear Friends and members of the family, it is humbling to be asked to deliver the funeral oration of one who was such a rare human being. Death is always a stranger until it invades your home and takes away a member of your family. As one who has recently lost his beloved daughter, I know how indescribably painful it is to lose a loved one.

Our hearts go out to Woizero Awetash and her three young children for their grievous loss. But Manna's loss is not only his immediate family's loss. As a great tegadalai who paid his dues in more ways than one, Manna belongs as much to the nation as he does to his

63

immediate family. Manna was my comrade-in-arms in many battles, and I respected him immensely. He was loved and respected by all who knew him and who had the honor to serve with him. He fulfilled, without fail, the freedom fighter's ethic "Let my comrade have the benefits before me, and let me die before my comrade." And Manna had a rare sense of humor that brightened the day even in the most desperate moments. He was a shining star among his comrades. In short, he was a model *tegadalai* in the true sense of the word.

[Some women freedom fighters begin to weep afresh and, with them, Awetash who is held from left and right by two relatives. Her eyes are red from crying].

THE PRIEST

[Borrowing the mike from Senai] Women of Asmara, shed no tears for him who has met his Maker. Shed tears for yourselves. Let the speaker continue his oration, I beg you.

SENAI

What makes Manna's death even more painful is that he was killed in captivity by members of the security forces who took the law into their hand and executed him. He had committed no crime. His crime, if it can be called that, was his honesty, integrity and his determination to keeping the faith. He took a stand against all odds, to continue to live by the promise of the revolution for which we all fought and for which our martyrs gave their lives and our disabled veterans gave their limbs.

[Andu appears suddenly surrounded by a dozen uniformed police and makes his way to within a hearing distance of Senai. Senai surveys the uniformed policemen. He knew that his remarks were provocative and broke from his past mode of operation and the agreement with his fellow dissidents. But he couldn't help it, he had passed the threshold of tolerance, particularly after his daughter's death. Two of the fellow dissidents, Zaghir and Hagaz are disturbed when they see the appearance of Andu and his uniformed police entourage].

SENAI

Dear friends and comrades of Manna, I must ask you to remember Manna, and we are gathered here to pay our last homage to him. For now, at least, let us put aside our specific grievances out of respect for Senai. Let us honor his memory by separating the issues and focusing our attention on parting from him with our love and respect. Le us also remember his grieving family and that we are here to share their grief. Now, before I turn over the mike to the reverend father to conclude the burial ceremony with a blessing, I have an announcement to make. I would like to inform all present that a few of us have decided to establish a Memorial Trust in Manna's name. My friend Kifle, who is visiting from America and who offered to establish a Memorial in my daughter' name has agreed, at my request, to make the donation, instead, to the Manna Memorial Trust. My family and I are deeply grateful for Kifle's generous offer, but we think it is more fitting to establish it in Manna's name. The first beneficiaries of the Trust will be Manna's children. It will go to help them in their education and sustenance. It will also help other needy children of martyrs.

[A general murmur of approval reverberates throughout the assembled mourners. Many ask to know who this Kifle is. Some voice sentiments of approval. Some women invoke the name of the Virgin Mary, asking her to bless him. The disabled veterans express words of interrogation which sound like discordant notes in the symphony of approbation].

AN UNIDENTIFIED
MAN

Why is he doing it now? What are his motives? I mean why didn't he do it to the hundreds of others before?

[These words were greeted with a massive sound of disapproval and the man looks towards Andu for guidance, but does not get it. Andu, like good opportunist, respects timing. He decides to let this pass for now].

SENAI

[Addressing the person who asked those questions] Why are you asking these questions? Here is a man who is offering his money for a cause. Nobody forced him to do it. There are no financial or other benefits accruing to him for doing what he proposes to do, and you are asking for his motives? You should be ashamed of yourself. Now place control yourself and have the decency to respect the memory of the departed and the grief of his family and friends. If you have ulterior motives for this absurd intervention, say so.

ANDU

[Coming to the defense of his man and trying to dilute Senai's eloquent speech] Don't forget that he was shot while killing another man, and an equally respected veteran *tegadalai* at that.

DISABLED VETERAN

Yes, and he is being buried with full honors while Manna is denied the same honor. Now what do you

	have to say to that? Your hero, Teklu, is hardly buried and you are hot in pursuit of his title and office, you ambitious bastard!
ANDU	Why you miserable creep. *[He is intercepted by two mourners before going to attack the disabled veterans. Senai appeals for calm and the officiating priest takes over the mike].*
PRIEST	Dear friends, we need to remember the words of the Prince of Peace in regard to forgiveness. Everyone affected by the tragic events that claimed the lives of two veterans and all of us will do well to remember the words of our Savior. I ask you again to bow your heads in humility as we offer our last prayers for the salvation of the souls of the departed. Amen and go in peace.
	[The mourners begin to leave the hilly burial ground and slowly make their ways towards the open field outside the entrance of the cemetery. There, the family of Manna—his wife and oldest daughter, their closest relatives, joined by Senai, Kifle and a few of Senai's fellow dissidents line up against the wall of the cemetery's external wall. The mourners approach them in small groups and murmur words of condolences and walk away. This ceremony goes on for at least a half-hour after which the deceased's family and friends start leaving, and the assembly of thousands of mourners disperse. Senai and his friends are walking behind Awetash and her relatives when Andu followed by an entourage of ten police men in uniform block their way and surround them, cutting them from the retinue of relatives of the deceased. They waited until they reached the narrow pass that led from the open filed to the motor road beyond. But there were still many people who had stayed behind to let the relatives go first and who witnessed this surprising development. One of these is Sister Delores who had heard his funeral oration and followed him from a distance].
SENAI	What the hell are you doing?
ANDU	Dr. Senai, you are under arrest. And please don't make fuss or try to resist the arrest.
SENAI	What do you mean I am under arrest? What right do you have to arrest me and at such a time and please? Have you no shame? On whose authority are you arresting me?

ANDU	Never mind who authorized the arrest. We have the power to arrest you. That's all that counts.
SENAI	You do not have the right to arrest me. I am an MP, a member of the National Assembly. I can only be arrested on the authority of a majority vote of the members of the National Assembly, unless I am caught red-handed, committing a crime.
ANDU	Tell that to the judges.
SENAI	What judges? And speaking of judges, do you know that you are required by the law to obtain a warrant of arrest under a judge's signature?
ANDU	Senai, your precious National Assembly approved the detention of your colleagues a few weeks ago, and you were part of those decisions. What right do you have to claim a privilege that you denied others? Isn't that hypocritical of you?

[Andu shoves Senai forward to indicate that he was in control and that Senai was under his power. He then calls one of the uniformed policemen to bring the prison van nearer. He does all this smiling and chuckling with pleasure. Senai does not find it necessary to tell him that he did not approve of the Resolution condemning innocent veteran fighters, and that his protests fell on deaf ears. Andu signals one of the uniformed police who takes out a something out of his pocket and proceeds to handcuff Senai, whereupon a murmur of protest comes from the observing public. One of the members of Senai's entourage whom another uniformed police tried to handcuff resists the arrest and is struck with a police baton on the back and the groin. He doubles over and falls to the ground. Senai tells everyone to stay calm and do as Andu asks. He and a couple of others are led away by the police to the general consternation of the people who had stayed behind to observe what was happening. Before they are led into the van Senai turns round and notices Sister Delores who stands with her hands in a prayer pose and smiles at him as if to say "Courage; this too shall pass." Senai smiles back and then turns to Andu].

SENAI	Andu, You have not an ounce of decency in you. Do you remember when you used to beg me to put in a good word for you with the Boss? You used to go out of your way to bow and scrape to get promotion. Have you forgotten all that?

ANDU	Wake up Senai. That was then, this is now. Now I am in charge of the security after Teklu's demise, and look where you are! Don't blame me for what you brought upon yourself. You should be happy with the privileges that you enjoy and obey higher authority. That is my guiding principle obey higher authority and enjoy your privileges. *[He laughs and orders his subordinate to take the prisoners and move. Then Kifle charges forward furiously and addresses Andu].*
KIFLE	I want to know where you are taking them, and I know my rights.
ANDU	Shut up, you CIA agent?
KIFLE	You can't frighten me by intimidation. I know I am not a CIA agent as you charge. Now, I repeat where are you taking them? I am a friend of Senai's and I want to know where you are taking him. His family will also want to know the same thing.
ANDU	Okay, Mr. Human Rights Advocate, you will have your answer. My answer to you is you'd be better off without knowing where we are taking them or what will happen to them.
KIFLE	That is a typical political terror, but it won't work with me, and I warn you that you will answer for these illegal arrests. A day will come when you cannot hide behind a claim of superior orders.
	[Andu leaves him and takes off to catch up with the other security men who are shepherding the arrested men toward a waiting van. Sister Delores approaches Kifle and tells him she too is a friend of the family].
SISTER DELORES	I admire you for what you just told that man. I too want to know where they are taking them. We must find out where they took them, quickly.
KIFLE	Yes, but how?
SISTER DELORES	I know how. I have a way of finding out.
KIFLE	*[Puzzled and admiring her spirit]* Who are you really? Could it be that you are using the nun's habit as disguise. How do I know I can trust you?
SISTER DELORES	The habit is genuine, but my work covers matters that are not purely spiritual. That is all I can say.
KIFLE	Then let us proceed to find out. *[They leave together].*

ACT FOUR

Sacrifice and Redemption

SCENE ONE

[In a Prison Camp at an undisclosed location. It is late afternoon in late April. The place could be anywhere in the Sahel region in the north of the country, judging by the flora and fauna.

Looking at this horseshoe shaped valley from the narrow entrance point, one is impressed by the sheer heights of the steep hills encircling it, which look like gigantic, man-made walls that no one can scale. The eerie sights and sounds— the strange variety of plants inhabiting this arid zone—reinforce the condition of hopelessness weighing heavily on the spirit of any one arriving for the first time. The raucous sound of some of the birds is anything but music to the ear. And then there are the desert plants, perched on the top of the rocks that encircle the valley—the dwarf shrubs stunted by millennial struggle to survive in the searing heat. These appear, from the distance, like grim sentinels looking down on, and mocking the prisoners below.

Little wonder then that the powers-that-be, ever resourceful in their will to punish, discipline and control, chose this place as a "reeducation camp." It is being used with a view to breaking the spirit of any one dissenting from or opposed to their policies. The camp is under the constant watch of a platoon of armed guards who work on shifts. No one can escape from this place. This afternoon, a group of guards are whiling the hours away, playing a card game and drinking tea. Others are sleeping under the shade of makeshift tents, open on all four sides. The leader of the camp, who had his walkie-talkie on, suddenly gets up from the card game. He calls the guard on duty at the top of one of the strategic hills.]

CAMP LEADER	Hello Zagrey...Hello Zagrey...Do you read me?
GUARD ON DUTY	I can hear you. Did you receive my message?
CAMP LEADER	Yes, I received it; that is why I am calling now. How many vehicles can you see coming?
GUARD ON DUTY	I can see five.
CAMP LEADER	Can you identify what type of cars they are?
GUARD ON DUTY	I can see two, four-wheel drive Toyotas. The rest are behind a cloud of dust and I cannot make out what make they are. I have trained my binoculars on them waiting to see if the dust settles. It will be easier when they turn round the bend in the road.
CAMP LEADER	Good. Keep looking and let me know of any details.
GUARD ON DUTY	Will do.
CAMP LEADER	Okay. Over and out. [*Turning to his deputy*] Five Toyotas! This must be a big visit, and we don't have enough provisions to entertain VIPs. Do we have much drink in the secret store?
DEPUTY	We have plenty of beer, thanks to General Chuchu's last visit. I wish they could all come with boxes of beer, like good old Chuchu. Chuchu is great. Whatever they say about his wild ways and petty trading, at least he does not forget those of us in trenches.
CAMP LEADER	Chuchu is a shrewd operator. What he is doing in all these seemingly generous gestures is buying an insurance policy in case of a future showdown. He showers selected officers and men in strategic places with gifts of beer and other goodies.
DEPUTY	Then why don't the others do the same?
CAMP LEADER	First, because they don't understand insurance policy as Chuchu does. Second, because they are mean and selfish bastards.
DEPUTY	[*With a broad grin*]. Now, at last, you are talking my language. They are all treacherous bastards who have forgotten their oaths and betrayed their trust.
CAMP LEADER	Be careful, I warn you. You repeat that kind of language in front of others, and you'll join the inmates in there [*pointing to the valley*].
DEPUTY	I never talk this way in front of others, except to one or two like you whom I can trust.
CAMP LEADER	[*Annoyed*]. Trust? How do you know you can trust

anybody, these days? How do you know you can trust me? I can't even trust myself, if that makes any sense.

DEPUTY   I just know. Besides, there are times when men must take risks. Otherwise, we would be paralyzed and subject to cynical manipulation by those who govern us. After all, we didn't spend our youth fighting for freedom only to be enslaved by fear, reduced to a bunch of frightened goons.

CAMP LEADER   [Irritable]. You amaze me. Despite all the hardships you have been through, you are still a true believer. I must say, I admire you for that. But, for God's sake, stop preaching to me.

DEPUTY   Well, you provoked me.

                [Sound of walkie-talkie] Hello Central Command. Do you hear me?

CAMP COMMANDER I hear you Zagre. Go ahead.

GUARD ON DUTY   Vehicles approaching Camp. They are about two miles away. By the way, they are all Toyotas. And the first car is flying a flag.

CAMP COMMANDER What kind of flag?

GUARD ON DUTY   How many kinds are there?

CAMP COMMANDER You son of a bitch!

GUARD ON DUTY   [Laughing] You are a better son of a bitch.

CAMP COMMANDER Tell me when they are within four or five hundred meters away. Over and out. [Excitedly and turning to deputy] A flag!

DEPUTY   A flag? Aha! Are you thinking what I am thinking?

CAMP COMMANDER Maybe. Then have a quick check of the guesthouse. It was thoroughly cleaned but just have another look in case there is need to remove or add something there for the use by the guest. See to it that there is enough water in the cistern for shower. That is the first thing they are going to ask for.

                [The Deputy Commander complies by passing on the order to other guards who were standing a little distance away.]

                [Walkie talkie calls] Hello Central Command. They are here, only some five hundred meters away. They should be at your gate in a matter of minutes.

CAMP LEADER   Thanks Zagrey. We are ready for them.

GUARD ON DUTY	You'd better be, because if you are not, all hell will be let loose on your head. Ha! Ha! Ha! Ha!
CAMP LEADER	You baboon!
GUARD ON DUTY	[*Still laughing*] Likewise.
DEPUTY	Where does all that laughter come from?
CAMP LEADER	He is demented.
DEPUTY	Aren't we all, for God's sake! This place can make anybody go mad. When will it all end? When are we going home to our families? We are as much prisoners as those we are guarding. Do you know that I am forgetting the names of my children? Is there a way out of this hellish place?
CAMP LEADER	You are asking the wrong man. You will have a chance to ask some of the VIPs who will be with us soon. Speak of the devil and…Here they come.
	[*Presently, the first vehicle stops outside the gate. The other cars also are parked behind the first car and people start jumping out of some of them. The occupants of th second and fifth cars are armed soldiers. They stand guard around the third and fourth cars. The driver of the first car goes round the front of the car to open the door. And out comes, a tall figure wearing a khaki shirt, kaki cap to match it, jeans trousers and sunglasses. The other occupants of the vehicle move towards the tall man and form a semi-circle around him. His head towers over all the others. When he walks, they walk; when he stops, they stop. And, as if he is enjoying seeing them do this, he repeats the ritual of walking short steps and stopping as they follow suit. The Camp Leader goes to meet them and he is greeted coldly by the tall man, though the others shake his hand, and a couple even give him the traditional shoulder touching and squeezing.*]
TALL MAN	[*Surveying his surroundings and gazing at the valley, addresses the Camp Leader*] Where are the other guards? Is this all you have?
CAMP LEADER	There are a few more who are doing production duties.
TALL MAN	What kind of duties?
CAMP LEADER	They are gathering firewood.
TALL MAN	Why don't you use prison labor for that?
CAMP LEADER	We do. But somebody has to guard the prisoners as they gather wood.

TALL MAN	Perhaps you think you re scoring a point. You are not. You said, "they are doing production duties." Those were your exact words. Yes or no? *[Camp Leader lowers his head in deference mixed with fear]*. You should have said, they are on duty guarding prisoners who are gathering firewood. Right?
CAMP LEADER	Right.
DEPUTY	Excuse my intrusion, comrade, but what is the difference? They are doing production duties indirectly when they guard those who are engaged in gathering wood. It is division of labor to the same end—gathering wood. Isn't it?
TALL MAN	Is it?
DEPUTY	Isn't it?
	[The Tall Man stares at the Deputy. It is eye-ball to eye-ball for a moment, and the Deputy refuses to look away and be stared down].
Tall Man	Who are you? And I don't remember addressing my questions to you.
DEPUTY	I am the Deputy Camp Leader and I waited for the comrade Camp Leader to answer your question. When he didn't I decided to answer it. Is it forbidden for a comrade to speak his mind? That was not the case during the struggle. Do you remember?
TALL MAN	Yes I do remember. Thank you for reminding me. We can easily forget, can't we? And I admire your guts. *[Turning to the Camp Leader]* We have special guests for you today. I hope you can accommodate them.
CAMP LEADER	We have enough rooms, but some of the guests may have to sleep in the same room. They are large rooms.
TALL MAN	I don't think you understand what I am talking about. We have prisoners that are dangerous and have to be under continual watch.
CAMP LEADER	I see. I thought you were referring to the company of guests who accompanied you. Now I understand. We have enough room to take in as many as fifty inmates.
TALL MAN	Good. Mind you, these new ones have to be kept separate from all the others. *[Pointing to one of the officials who came in his car]* Do you see the young man with the sun glasses? He will fill you in with the details. *[Signals the young man with the sun glasses to come along and*

the young man joins them] You two have a lot to talk about. You know the guidelines on the processing of the prisoners, so explain to the Camp Leader in detail. [*He stresses the word "processing" and the young man nods as does the Camp Leader*]. So, make sure that it is done according to the guidelines. No mistakes of any kind, no relaxation of the rules will be tolerated. Understood?

CAMP LEADER   Understood.

TALL MAN   [*Pulling the Camp Leader away and lowering his voice*] By the way, how long has your deputy been here with you?

CAMP LEADER   Almost from the beginning, which is now eight years.

TALL MAN   I like his guts. He deserves a raise.

CAMP LEADER   We all do, I think. Deserve a raise I mean.

TALL MAN   Yes, but his kind of guts should be specially rewarded. [*He leaves him to join the company of his entourage and talks to the young man with the glasses*] Did you hear what the Deputy Camp Leader said to me?

YOUNG MAN   No. What did he say?

TALL MAN   Never mind what he said. He is dangerous. Get his dossier and report to me about him, immediately. Ask the Camp leader to give you his dossier, but don't tell him why you want it.

YOUNG MAN   Yes sir.

TALL MAN   Now get the prisoners out of the cars and take them in. They are to go in the same way they came—blind folded. They are to see no one and talk to no one. Understood?

YOUNG MAN   Yes sir. Two of them have been sick, and have been asking for medicines and to see doctors. What shall we do?

TALL MAN   What is wrong with them?

YOUNG MAN   One is a diabetic and has hyper tension. The other is asthmatic and has ulcers.

TALL MAN   Tell them we will be sending for a helicopter with a doctor to treat them in a couple of days. That should keep them quiet. Now go and take them to their new quarters. The Camp Leader will show you where. And tell the Deputy Camp Leader to come here.

[*On his way to order the prisoners out of the cars and taken to their new abode, the young man tells the*

Deputy Camp Leader he is wanted by the chief guest. He then orders the prisoners to move towards the end of the valley.]

DEPUTY

Did you ask for me?

TALL MAN

Yes. I want to give you a special assignment. Do you see the new prisoners being taken to their new abode?

DEPUTY

Yes I do.

TALL MAN

Well, I want you to be a special liason with them, to befriend them and appear to be sympathetic to their cause. [*He pauses and watches the Deputy's reaction*]. Can you do that?

DEPUTY

As a soldier, I will follow orders, of course. But I don't know who they are and what their cause is. They are being led blind folded. I assume there is good reason for doing that.

TALL MAN

[*Repeats the Deputy's words verbatim, laaughing loudly, almost hysterically*] " I assume there is good reason for doing that." I like that. Hey, you are good. And you assume right.

Suddenly, a loud voice is heard from the direction of the blind folded and shackled prisoners who are being shepherded towards the end of the valley.

THE VOICE

I know that laughter. My eyes are blindfolded, but my ears are not stuffed. So you came with us. I can tell you are here from hearing your voice. Why are you hiding? Why did you travel with u all the way incognito? Are you afraid even when we are under your boots? You came with your prisoners all the way from Asmara, and yet you did not let your voice heard. You honor us too much, great Chief.

TALL MAN

[*To the young man with the sunglasses*] Bring him here. Let the others wait.

[*The owner of the voice is almost as tall as the man who summoned him. Now he stands blindfolded facing the Tall Man and the Deputy*].

PRISONER

[*Standing face to face with the Tall Man*] Let me see, how many meters am I standing from where you are standing, or are you sitting?

TALL MAN

Never mind that. [*To the young man*] You can take off his blind folds. [*When the young man takes off the blind folds, the prisoner shuts his eyes which canot stand the light after two days being in the dark*]

TALL MAN	Now, tell me. What difference does it make whether you knew that I was in your convoy or not?
PRISONER	[*Squinting and not able to see closing his eyes and laughing*] I would have enjoyed our chat. Do you remember the chats we used to have on our trips to and from the highlands during the war? I miss that.
TALL MAN	Always sarcastic, even in captivity.
PRISONER	Well that is something you can't take away from me. And by the way, why this ridiculous blind fold? I mean, we know we cannot escape from Sahel prisons, after all, we used to be on the captors' side of the fence in those days. This reversal of fortune in which we find ourselves is becoming ludicrous every day.
TALL MAN	You brought it on yourself. I didn't
PRISONER	No, you brought it on us. You had been waiting for an opportune moment to harvest the next crop of victims to quench your insatiable thirst for absolute power. Our mistake was in believing you would listen to reason.
TALL MAN	I always listen to reason. But I can't stand lies and excuses. Your accusation of my appetite for power, for instance, is a bald lie. I hold power in the name of the people. I embody the will of the masses; the masses are with me because I am with them and for them.
PRISONER	The poor masses—how much crime has been committed in their name! But let's leave the masses for the moment. I want to know why this theatrics of blindfolding and shackles? It is more comical than tragic. Where do you think we would fly to, if we were not shackled and blind folded? Don't you think it is ludicrous. You must agree, you used to have a wry sense of humor. Have you lost that too?
TALL MAN	What do you mean "that too"? What else have I lost?
PRISONER	You have lost your sense of right and wrong. You lost it a long time ago when we let you do whatever you wanted. We are to blame for letting you do whatever you wanted. But it reached its maximum—you became like Napoleon—when you ignored the rest of us, including the representatives of your beloved masses and decided to go it alone in the Weyane-Eritrean war.
TALL MAN	[*Clearly losing his temper*] I did not go it alone. The Party was with me all the way, except a few traitors like you. And now even loyal members like Dr. Senai have joined you. Where is he by the way?

PRISONER	He is very ill. He has been calling for medical care throughout the journey, and no one would listen or care about his agony.
TALL MAN	He'll get medical attention tomorrow, or the day after.
PRISONER	What if he dies in the meantime?
TALL MAN	[*Sotto voce*] The traitor—let him die, do I care?
PRISONER	Even traitors have a right to medical care. By the way, if you believe in the fabricated lies, the mantra of "traitors…traitors," why don't you bring us to face trial in court. That is what is done in civilized societies. You are civilized aren't you? So, why were you afraid of charging us in open court? I'll tell you why. You don't have a shred of evidence to support your ridiculous charge of treason. I dare you to bring us to court instead of shuffling us from one prison camp to another.
TALL MAN	Why are you in a hurry to be judged. We have enough evidence to hang you. But we are in no hurry.
PRISONER	You don't have evidence and you know it. I know you; if you had evidence you would have had us paraded in open court—not in your special court, but in open court. As for your claim that the party was behind you in the Weyane dispute, I am a member of the Party's Central Council and I do not remember a meeting that decided on this issue. What you call Party consists of your handpicked yes-men who do your bidding.
TALL MAN	I know your ambition, you son of a bitch. You wanted the Presidential Chair and conspired to dispatch me in a coup. But I was too quick for you.
PRISONER	To power hungry people like you everyone conspires to take away their position. If you only knew how much I was tired of politics. All I wanted was a peaceful life to raise my children. But I could not sit tight as you took the country down the drain. So I protested. That is my only crime.
TALL MAN	[*Calling the man with the sun glasses*] Away with him.

[*The tall man goes to meet the rest of his entourage who were being taken to their quarters with some of the guards carrying their bags and other belongings.*

All the while, the Deputy Camp Commander was keenly following, from a safe distance, the incredible dialogue going on between two big people. He now approaches the Camp Commander.]

DEPUTY COMMANDER	What was that all about? Who is the prisoner?
CAMP COMMANDER	How could you forget him? He is one of the heroes of the armed struggle. If any one individual could claim any decisive role in the achievement of victory against incredible odds, during our war of liberation, he can.
DEPUTY COMMANDER	What a marvelous way to treat a hero! What a wonderful country! I should escape from this place and go to the Sudan or anywhere.
CAMP COMMANDER	I wouldn't be in a hurry if I were you; not before you get a salary raise.
DEPUTY COMMANDER	What salary raise?
COMMANDER	Didn't the Chief tell you? He was so impressed by your boldness, he said you deserve a raise.
DEPUTY COMMANDER	And what did you say?
COMMANDER	I said we all deserve a raise.
DEPUTY COMMANDER	And he singled me out for a raise, right? *[The Commander nods in assent]* I smell a rat. It confirms my suspicion. Do you know what he told me? He said he wants me to act as if I believe in the cause of the prisoners and spy on them and report to him.
COMMANDER	Are you going to?
DEPUTY COMMANDER	Of course. But feed him information damaging to them? Hell, no.
COMMANDER	Now listen. All this didn't happen. I have not heard anything. You have not told me anything. Okay?
DEPUTY COMMANDER	Scared, huh? Well don't worry; I won't squeal on you. This man is incredible, though, isn't he? It is the first time I came face to face with him. I have never liked him, but I sort of gave him the benefit of the doubt. Well, now no benefit of the doubt. He is a double-faced intriguer, a real monster. He tells you one thing and he tells another something else.
COMMANDER	How do you think he has remained on top for so long. As they say in America, it goes with the territory.

DEPUTY COMMANDER	What goes with the territory?
COMMANDER	Double-faced intrigue.
DEPUTY COMMANDER	Well, it is not for me.
COMMANDER	That's why you are not the Chief. Let's go and meet our masters. [*They laugh and start moving towards the guesthouse*].

SCENE TWO

[*Inside the prisoners' quarters. Evening of the same day.*

The new prisoners have been settled in their new abodes. The VIPs have done with their carousing and gone to sleep. It is after midnight, and the Deputy Camp Commander is taking Snai's temperature, sitting beside him. Senai is lying on a worn out mattress on the ground. Two other prisoners, including the one who had a run-in with the Chief are also lying on the ground.]

DEPUTY	You certainly have fever. By the way, I am the unofficial barefoot doctor in this camp. That was my first job when I joined the struggle in the late seventies. I still remember the names of diseases and the medicines for those diseases. I even conducted minor operations on the frontline after some battles. So, I will do what I can for you until a real doctor comes
SENAI	[*Coughing and clutching his chest in pain*] If a doctor comes you mean.
DEPUTY	We have been assured by the Chief that a helicopter will come, carrying a doctor and medicines, in a day or two.
ANOTHER PRISONER	[*Laughing*] The country doesn't have a helicopter, and he says he will send one with a doctor and medicines to serve prisoners. If you believe that you will believe the Brooklyn Bridge is for sale, as the Americans would say.
SENAI	[*Although in pain, doing his best to put up a brave front*] Actually, the Brooklyn Bridge is up for sale these days. I read that in Time Magazine.
THE OTHER PRISONER	If you believe everything you read in the Press, you will believe anything, including the promise of a helicopter service to prisoners.

DEPUTY	Well, here is a pill that should ease your pain. Take it twice a day, one in the morning, one in the evening, after meals. I believe you have pneumonia. I will need some antibiotic and we have some stored for special occasions. I don't see why we shouldn't consider your coming here as a special occasion. [*Laughter*].
THE TALL PRISONER	I like this guy. I think we will be better off here than we have been in Asmara and its environs.
DEPUTY	Well, you keep saying that and they will send me packing to join you guys here.
TALL PRISONER	We don't want that. But thanks anyway for your kindness.
DEPUTY	Listen, don't thank me. It is your right. You don't deserve to be here and certainly not brought in the manner you were brought here, blindfolded and shackled. No human being, certainly no veteran who spent his youth fighting for freedom, should be treated this way. But, I repeat, please keep your feelings to yourselves.
TALL PRISONER	We will, indeed. Thank you.
DEPUTY	Well, Good night, I'll see you tomorrow.
PRISONERS	[*in unison*] Good night.

[*Senai stays awake for several hours after the Deputy's visit. The other two prisoners fall asleep. As one of them snores, Senai tosses on the mattress, blocking his ears with the parts of his towel, which he brought with him. As there is no roof over the desert dungeon to which he and his companions had been consigned, he can see the stars in the wide-open sky, and the dark outlines of the peaks of the rocks surrounding the valley. Then the fading stars gave way to a pallor heralding the morning to come. He had spent a whole night without sleep. But somewhere he began to hear the faint throbbing of sound of a ghostly kirar music, palpitating on the same note endlessly. He recognized it as the song Wedi TiKul made popular during the armed struggle in the 1980's. He focuses his mind on the music, which gradually dominates the snoring sound. Eventually, he falls asleep and starts dreaming.*

In his dreams he is part of a music festival in which several musicians play, sometimes as a symphony, at other times separately. Among the prominent competitors is Wedi TiKul and his songs win out in the end, taking over all the others, as he struts on the stage playing on his Kirar.]

In the dream, Wedi TiKul acts not only as musician, but as a battalion commander. His troops march in lockstep to his music and fire away at the invisible enemy across a dark valley. Senai who acts as the commissar of the battalion, tries to stop the troops from firing without target, but his plea falls on deaf ears.]

SENAI WEDI TIKUL,   Why don't you stop them from shooting aimlessly and wasting ammunition?

WEDI TIKUL   *[Continuing to play his Kirar, answers Senai in song, smiling at him with affection]*

O Senai, Senai, Senai!

You gentle Tegadalai,

How can you stop Gombel?

O Senai, Senai, Senai!

You exemplary Tegadalai!

How can you stop Gombel?

Gombel is in a race with destiny.

How can you stop Gombel,

In his race with destiny?

O Senai, Senai, Senai!

You gentle Tegadalai!

O Senai, Senai, Senai!

You hero of heroes,

Let Gombel meet his destiny,

In this, his finest hour.

O Senai...Senai...Senai...

You gentle Tegadalai...

[Suddenly, three men carrying Kalashniko assault rifles (Kalashin), appear from the middle of nowhere, riding in a four-wheel drive Toyota. They jump out of the car, surround Wedi TiKul and tell him he is under arrest. Two of them tie his hands behind his back and push him towards the car. The third approaches Senai and asks for his ID card.]

SENAI   I don't have an ID card. I didn't know we need to carry ID cards.

1st Kalashin Man	Well now you know. What is your name?
Senai	Dr. Senai Embaie.
Kalashin Man	To which unit do you belong?
Senai	The Department of Economy.
Kalashin Man	Then what are you doing here, with these criminals?
Senai	Who are the criminals? I thought I was in the company of fellow freedom fighters.
Kalashin Man	The enemy has infiltrated us. You can't be too careful, these days. Since you don't carry an ID card, can anyone vouchsafe for you, for your true identity?
Senai	Wedi TiKul knows me and where I work. You can ask him.
Second Kalashin Man	[*Laughing*] That is ridiculous. Wedi TiKul is under arrest and is not entitled to give testimony on anybody's behalf.
Senai	Then arrest me too and take me to the Security Department; someone is sure to know me and confirm my identity.
Second Kalashin Man	[*Having consulted the other two and turning to Senai*] Okay, let's go.

[*Senai joins Wedi TuKul in the back of the Toyota, but his hands are left untied. They drive up a hill along a winding track road, called Bidiho, passing several groups of fighters walking in the opposite directions. No one greets them or makes any gesture of greeting. At last, they arrive at a clearing on top of a hill, and are told to get out of the Toyota. They are taken to a wooded place higher up on the hill where they see a crowd of people sitting on the ground. Three black-robed men with black caps are sitting on an elevated ground above the crowd. The one sitting in the middle who sits slightly above the other two, is a bearded man with a long face and aquiline nose. A stone hewn out of a rock serves as the desk of the judges.*]

First Kalashin Man	Your honor, here is the arch criminal, known as Wedi TiKul, who has been corrupting our *Yikalo tegadelti*.
Chief Judge	In what way has he been corrupting our youth?

FIRST KALASHIN MAN	With music your honor. Especially the young women *tegadelti* have started worshipping him as a cult figure. This is not only counter-revolutionary, it is downright corrupt and philistine.
THIRD JUDGE	Did he say Palestinians? Has the criminal been consorting with Palestinians, and thereby compromising the purity of our revolution?
SECOND JUDGE	I believe he said philistine, which is a different thing.
CHIEF JUDGE	Why would music be a corrupting influence, please, Kalashin Man?
FIRST KALASHIN MAN	Our great leader thinks it is corrupting because it takes the mind away from the revolutionary duty. Besides, cult figures divert attention from the leader; we can only have one leader. Yes, one leader, one Party and one country.
CROWD	Hear! Hear!
CHIEF JUDGE	Quiet!
KALASHIN MAN	The criminal songster has bewitched our youth and uses his music to send them to their deaths for no purpose. He deserves a thousand deaths.
CROWD	Hear! Hear!
WEDI TIKUL	Even if I die, I can only die once.
CROWD	Hear! Hear!
CHIEF JUDGE	I said quiet. Any more disturbance like that and I will hold you all in contempt and send you down to pick firewood from the valley yonder.
WEDI TIKUL	Your honor, may I answer these ridiculous charges?
THIRD JUDGE	How can you call them ridiculous if they are true?
WEDI TIKUL	That is precisely the point; they are not true, and therefore they are ridiculous.
THIRD JUDGE	If the Kalashin Man who is an honorable revolutionary, says they are true, then in revolutionary logic, they are true.
WEDI TIKUL	Then what is the point of appearing before judges. I mean if the Kalashin Man, who is acting as police and prosecutor is also deciding on the truth and falsity of an issue in dispute, then what is your role as judges.

THIRD JUDGE	My mind is made up, don't confuse me with sophisticated arguments.
SECOND JUDGE	The accused has a point, there.
THIRD JUDGE	Whose side are you on?
SECOND JUDGE	On the side of truth and justice.
THIRD JUDGE	I resent your insinuation.
CHIEF JUDGE	Gentlemen, gentlemen. Order please. You are detaining us with side issues. I, myself, am not persuaded that the charge of corrupting the youth with music is tenable.
KALASHIN MAN	Your honor, have you considered the consequences of going against the word of our great leader?
CHIEF JUDGE	I work on the assumption that our great leader stands for truth and justice I assume that he would not countenance the corruption of justice which is a far more insidious kind of corruption. Have I explained myself?
KALASHIN MAN	[*Sulking and grumbling*] You have to me, but I hope your explanation can stand the withering inquiry of His Excellency.
CHIEF JUDGE	Now let us proceed with the case of Wedi TiKul. Do you have anything else against this man?
KALASHIN MAN	No, sir. I rest my case.
CHIEF JUDGE	Then if I were his lawyer, in a proper proceedings, I would call for dismissal of the charges on the ground that there is no case to answer. I am ready dismiss the case.
	At that point, the Third judge approaches the Chief Judge and whispers in his ears. The Chief Judge's expression visibly changes, as if he was hit by a hammer.
CHIEF JUDGE	Then we shall retire to the bush and deliberate on our judgement.
	[*The third Judge smiles with satisfaction and the three judges rise and walk a few meters away where they are engaged in inaudible debate among themselves. Senai approaches the Chief Kalshin Man.*]
SENAI	May I ask you when you are going to submit my case?
KALASHIN MAN	As far as I know, there is no case against you. Yours is a matter of determining your identity. But we cannot let you go until some one attests to your true identity.

SENAI	And I say it is a serious offence against a person's humanity when a man is denied his identity. By what right do you refuse to believe me when I tell you who I am and what I do in our common struggle. The fact that you carry a Kalashin should not make you a judge over a person's destiny.
KALASHIN MAN	I am only following orders.
SENAI	Who authorized you to make arrests of people whose identity you cannot determine because you don't know them?
KALASHIN MAN	All I know is that a person who does not carry an ID card is to be brought to the authorities for the necessary action.
SEANI	Who issued the rule about the ID card? It is news to me, and I have been in the struggle before you.
KALASHIN	Ask the judges when they come back.
SENAI	I will, but I doubt if they have the power to do anything about it.
	[*The judges return and take their position on the stony bench, only this time it is the third judge who presides. Upon seeing that their favorite judge is now the presiding judge, the members of crowd explode into a wild cheer and applause. The new Chief Judge returns the favor by rising and bowing to the crowd. The former Chief judge looks dejected and has obviously been somehow or other intimidated, judging by his bowed head, which he does not lift to look at the parties or at the crowd. Senai whispers to Wedi TiKul.*]
SENAI	I am beginning to fear the worst. The least favorable judge has now been elevated to Chief Judge. Wasn't he the one who did not want to be confused by your arguments?
WEDI TIKUL	I am afraid so. The worst is yet to come. I don't like the newly elevated Chie Judge; I think he is after blood.
	[*The new Chief Judge clears his throat and calls the court to order.*]
CHIEF JUDGE	The prisoner will rise for the verdict.
KALASHIN MAN	Your honor, may I say something?
CHIEF JUDGE	What is it?
KALASHIN MAN	There is the matter of one Dr. Senai who was found without carrying the required ID card. He disputes the

	rule about ID cards and asks by whose authority we inquired into his identity and arrested him for failure to carry an ID card. What shall we do with him?
CHIEF JUDGE	Any man who does not carry and ID must be either a Rightist conspirator [a Yamin] or a Leftist conspirator [a Menka'e]—a conspirator against our leadership and its correct Mass line. [*Addressing Senai*] Which one of these conspirators do you belong to?
SENAI	I belong to neither. I am a free spirit who has always believed in the freedom of expression and of inquiry.
CHIEF JUDGE	That is bourgeois nonsense. There is no such thing as freedom of expression. All expressions must accord with the interests of the masses. Where did you get your education?
SENAI	In Asmara and later, in Italy.
CHIEF JUDGE	Well, you need to go to the reeducation camp to learn the mass line. [*Turning to the Kalashin Man*] Take him away and induct him in the proper school.
SECOND KALASHIN MAN	Come on Dr. Senai, we will take you to a different school where you will get another kind of doctorate. It will make you more humble; you will submit to the will of the masses.
SENAI	I think you mean the will of the masses that is embodied in the Great Leader?
SECOND KALASHIN MAN	You are learning fast. You will do well in our school. [*Turning to the Chief Judge*] Shall I wait until you deliver your verdict on Wedi TiKul, so that I can take them both?
CHIEF JUDGE	You will not have to wait too long. Here is the verdict. The accused shall rise. [*Wedi TiKul rises*] We, the revolutionary committee on justice, sentence you, TeKle Kifle-Mariam, also known as Wedi TiKul, to an indefinite period of incarceration with hard labor in the labor camp of the revolution.
	[*Someone from the crowd*] Excellent Verdict! Serves him right!
CHIEF JUDGE	There, in the labor camp, you will not be allowed to play your kirar or sing, even to yourself. Your songs are hereby judged to be offensive and corrupting and,

	therefore, prohibited. We hope you will learn humility and mend your ways. Your arrogance is one based on your talents. The arrogance of Dr. Senai is based on his so-called higher education. Now, if you show good behavior, you may be allowed to sing once a month. Take him away.
WEDI TIKUL	May I ask just one question?
CHIEF JUDGE	[*Impatiently*] What is it? Hurry up.
WEDI TIKUL	When this process began, the judge sitting on your right acted as the Chief Judge and you were the third judge. How did you switch roles and why is he keeping quiet now?
CHIEF JUDGE	He is quiet by nature.
WEDI TIKUL	He wasn't quiet before you took over. He was speaking his mind and he was fair. What happened in between?
CHIEF JUDGE	This is a matter of state secret and does not concern you.
WEDI TIKUL	It is a matter of judicial ethic and fairness, and as such it concerns me, since I am a party in the matter. I ask the former Chief Judge to answer me.
FORMER CHIEF JUDGE	First of all let me say how much I have enjoyed your songs over the years. They sustained me and others during critical times during our struggle. When I was acting as former Chief Judge earlier today, I had a lucid interval during which I was prepared to administer impartial justice. The lucid interval has now elapsed. That is all I can say, if I know what is good for me.
WEDI TIKUL	But I want to know what happened to change you?
CHIEF JUDGE	I had a relapse. I relapsed into the revolutionary mold of justice.
WEDI TIKUL	How so? Why so suddenly?
FORMER CHIEF JUDGE	As Confucius said, "Many are the ways of revolutionary justice and of Cochin China hens."
CHIEF JUDGE	There he goes again!
WEDI TIKUL	Could you explain what Confucius meant?
CHIEF JUDGE	He means if he had continued to administer justice in accordance with his conscience, he might have found himself in the same situation as you do now.

WDI TIKUL	But justice should be impartial.
CHIEF JUDGE	That is bourgeois justice
FORMER CHIEF JUDGE	*[Agitated and rising from his seat]* I can't take it any more. I must protest. I cannot take it any more. This is intolerable.
CHIEF JUDGE	Sit down and shut up!
FORMET CHIEF JUDGE	I will not sit down.
CHIEF JUDGE	Then remain standing.
FORMER JUDGE	I will not remain standing.
	[He walks down from the seat of judges moving past the crowd and into the wooded area. Even the hostile crowd is startled and confused. The Second Judge follows him and tries to persuade him to come back and, on failing to do so, counsels the Chief Judge to let him be.]
CHIEF JUDGE	Let him be? What does that mean? He is either with us or against us. Are you on his side too?
SECOND JUDGE	*[Frightened]* No, no. I am only worried that our revolutionary justice will get a bad press.
CHIEF JUDGE	Who cares about the press?
A MEMBER OF THE CROWD	Bravo Chief Judge of our revolution, bravo! Long live the revolution. Down with reactionaries and bourgeois intellectuals!
SENAI to WEDI TIKUL	It is with these kinds of sycophants that we have been bound. When will we be unbound?
	[As Senai and Wedi Tikul converse quietly, a member of the secret security who was sitting behind them listening rises and addresses the Chief Judge.]
SECURITY MAN	Your honor, I have something to report.
CHIEF JUDGE	What is it?
SECURITY MAN	The person who goes by the name of Dr. Senai and whose identity we don't recognize, has been whispering to the person known as Wedi TiKul.
CHIEF JUDGE	What were they saying?
SECURITY MAN	I did not hear all of it, but what I heard is disturbing.

CHIEF JUDGE	What did they say?
SECURITY MAN	Dr. Senai called the honorable members of the audience "sycophants." He also said that they are the ones, to quote him exactly, "who have bound us."
CHIEF JUDGE	Shackle him and tie his hands behind his back. Take them both away.
SECURITY MAN	And what shall we do with the dissenting judge who walked away from his revolutionary duty?
CHIEF JUDGE	You know what to do with him, I am sure.
SECURITY MAN	Yes, your honor, we do. I just wanted to make sure.
	[*The three Kalashin men and the secret security man approach Senai with a menacing look. As they begin to surround him, taking a handcuff and what Senai thinks is a knife, Senai shouts "don't come near me. I warn you." Then one of the Kalashin men draws a knife, raises it above his head and is about to strike at Senai's chest when Senai wakes up and bolts upright on his bed.*]
SENAI	Where are we?
FELLOW PRISONER	We are in a prison camp. Are you all right? You were crying, "Don't come near me." Were you having a nightmare?
SENAI	I was, an awful one.
FELLOW PRISONER	Well, we are all living a nightmarish existence. At least you woke up from yours. When will we wake up from this daily nightmare?
SENAI	Funny you say that. That was exactly what I was telling Wedi TiKul.
FELLOW PRISONER	Wedi TiKul?
SENAI	Yes, he was in my dream.
FELLOW PRISONER	At least you choose better company for your dreams. And how are you feeling, health-wise?
SENAI	I feel much better. I think the medicine our guardian angel gave me must have done the trick.
FELLOW PRISONER	I am glad. We were really concerned. Actually you look better already. When he gives you some anti-biotic, you will recover in no time.
SENAI	At least we must maintain our health to have a chance to fight another day. This looks like a long detention.
FELLOW PRISONER	Don't you believe it. The system has cracked, and once

	it has cracked it cannot be mended. It is a matter of time. Cheer up.
SENAI	Do I have a choice? [*laughter*].
FELLOW PRISONER	Just out of curiosity, who was the last witness who testified against you at the secret trial before the Special Court? You seemed to be surprised by his testimony.
SENAI	His name is Girmai. He was a fellow freedom fighter and a colleague at the Ministry where I worked. I wasn't completely surprised, but the extent of his lies was incredible. He leaned over backwards to say what they wanted him to say. He was my deputy at work, so he must have wanted my position very badly—the fool.
FELLOW PRISONER	Why do you say, "the fool?"
SENAI	Because the job he was coveting is meaningless. It is empty; it is just decorative.
FELLOW PRISONER	It may be decorative to you because you are a man of principle who wants to do something with the position. But he may be happy with a decorative position because that is his psychological make-up.
SENAI	Perhaps you are right. But I am amazed at the length to which some people can go for such pittance of a job. I mean I can understand a person who has children to raise wanting to keep a job, but coveting thy neighbor's job! Come to think of it, Moses should have included it as an Eleventh Commandment.
	[*At this point, the Deputy Camp Commander comes carrying a syringe and some vials.*]
DEPUTY	*Buon giorno dottore.* Good morning, good morning. Well, you look much better this morning. I have brought an anti-biotic in a vial; injection is more effective. I keep these things hidden in a special place for special guests. Six of these and you will be good and ready to go out to play football. Ha!ha!ha!.
SENAI	Thank you my friend. By the way where did you learn Italian?
DEPUTY	I lived in Italy until I joined the struggle. In fact, I remember seeing you at the Bologna Festival in the mid-seventies. It came back to me after I left you yesterday. You were much younger of course and you have changed a lot, as we all have.
SENAI	What brings you to this holiday spot?

DEPUTY	Well, it isn't exactly Livorno but, hey, we count our blessings. *E vero?*
SENAI	I like your attitude, but I am sure all this will be over soon, and we'll all look back on it and laugh it off. What makes me mad is the waste of human talent—the utter waste.
DEPUTY	Well, I have stopped thinking about those kinds of things. You have to, if you want to survive. You have to laugh—cynically, but laugh nonetheless. *Si tratta di sopravvivenza, caro dottore.* Well, I must go now. I'll see you later in the day.
SENAI	Thanks again.

[Exit Deputy Chief of Camp. Senai lies down to sleep.]

SCENE THREE

[In and around the Government Palace, a few days before the independence anniversary. Inside the Palace, a Press Conference is about to take place in the Hall of the Masses. The government Deputy Chief Protocol [DCP] is holding the fort to the assembled International Press Corps, pending the arrival of his Boss.]

DCP	Ladies and Gentlemen, Allow me, in the name of His Excellency, the President, to welcome you to the Hall of the Masses. His Excellency will join us in a moment, but while you are waiting I'd like to tell you something about the history of this place. I wish to remind you that when you ask your questions after His Excellency has made his statement, you need to identify not only yourself but what newspaper or other media you represent. And now, while waiting for the arrival of the President, I would like to tell you something about the history of this place.
THE POST REPRESENTATIVE	Why is it called the Hall of the Masses? The word "masses" smacks of communist ideology. Does your government still follow communist ideology?
DCP	The masses are the masses. Communism or no communism. Do you deny the existence of the masses?
POST REP	Excuse me I do the asking; I expect an answer from you. Does your government follow communist ideology or not—yes or no?

DCP	And I asked you, do you deny the existence of the masses—yes or no?
Post Rep	I will take your answer as an admission that your governmetn has not rejected communism.
Reuter Rep	Mr. Deputy Chief of Protocol, may I ask you another question?
DCP	Of course.
Reuter Rep	I have been talking to some Eritreans living abroad, in Europe and North America. Your government used to get a lot of assistance from the European Union, as well as remittances from Eritreans in the Diaspora. Two questions. First, how will your government fare in view of the threatened cut of EU aid, following Mr. Bandini's expulsion?
DCP	Mr. Bandini interfered in the internal affairs of Eritrea.
Reuter	I am sorry, I haven't finished my question. My second question is, why is your government forcing Eritreans abroad to pay two percent tax on their income? Is it true that they are denied the rights due to a citizen if they do not pay this tax and other dues? Let me just add that Ertreans friends asked me to raise these questions.
DCP	You can raise these questions to the proper authority.
AFP	You mean with the President?
DCP	Yes, if you want to.
AFP	I have another question for you about the name of this palace.
DCP	Not that again!
AFP	Since you wanted to tell us the history of the place, I remember reading somewhere that this palace was built by the Italians.
DCP	So was the city itself, so what?
AFP	I see no Italian name, such as the name of the first civilian governor to commemorate its proper history.
DCP	You mean like Palazzo Mazzini or Marconi, or…
AFP	Exactly.
DCP	No way. We have national heroes of our own. We don't celebrate colonialism; you may, but we don't, thank you very much.
AFP	It would be good for tourism. *[General Laughter]*.

DCP	Maybe, but there are some prices, which we are not willing to pay, even for tourism. *[Laughter].* ·
BBC	I want to take up again the issue of two percent tax Eritreans are required to pay as a condition for the provision of some services to which they are entitled as citizens of the country. Secondly, I want to know the status of the eleven political prisoners who were arrested in September last year. When are they going to appear in court?
DCP	You can ask the President. My role is to facilitate meetings, not to answer questions related to policy issues.
BBC	Why not? You strike me as an educated and highly sophisticated intellectual able to answer any question.
DCP	Flattery will get you nowhere. *[Laughter].*
BBC	I was not flattering you; you are an educated and highly.
DCP	I know, I know, "highly sophisticated intellectual." It is flattery because I know I am neither an intellectual nor sophisticated. I am just an average Joe who is doing his humble duty serving his nation the best way he can.
BBC	Well, let me put it this way. You ar an intelligent and articulate average Joe. *[Laughter].* And I happen to like you, having known you for a few years now.
DCP	*[Laughing]* You Brits are tenacious SOBs. I will allow you just one question; you must give the others a chance.

[Sounds of steps are heard echoing along the corridor leading to the hall. Presently, the door is opened; a security detail appears and surveys the assembled people, his eyes quickly scanning the Hall. Then a tall figure in a white open shirt and simple slacks and sandals appears and all the members of the Press Corps rise. He motions the audience to sit and takes his seat at the desk which carries a bowl of water, two glasses and the national flag placed at the center. The Deputy Chief of Protocol leans forward and whispers to his ear. He nods and prepares to speak by taking out a piece of paper from his shirt pocket. The President begins reading from a written text while seated.]

"Good morning ladies and gentlemen. I have a statement to make and then I will answer your questions. My statement will be very brief. I will address three main issues of current significance and of great interest to all of us. The first issue I wish to address concerns the boundary dispute between Eritrea and Ethiopia. You all remember that some two months ago now, the Hague Commission on the boundary dispute between the two countries came out with a verdict. Both parties to the dispute agreed at Algiers to be bound by the decision of the Commission. We accept the verdict and congratulate the people of Eritrea and Ethiopia, for they are the true winners. The second issue I want to address concerns the demobilization program for our armed forces and the financial support we need to carry out the program in the next few years. The third issue I want to address is our policy of self-reliance, which many foreign observers have misunderstood…"

[Suddenly a loud uproar is heard outside the building. The President looks at the security detail and as the uproar is repeated with resounding echoes in the building, two of the security officers rush out of the hall. A third goes to the window adjacent to the side of the building from which the noise came. As he opens the window the noise increases and the Press Corps rush to the window to see what is happening. The Deputy Chief of Protocol pleads with them to go back to their seats and looks at the President for guidance. The President joins the journalists to see what is going on. Upon discovery that the crowd outside may be a source of disturbance, he decides to postpone the Press Conference. He summons the DCP and tells him to announce to the Press Corps that the meeting will take place another day and walks out as unceremoniously as he came in.]

AFP   [To the AP man] He does not respect ceremony does he?

AP   Well, I would do the same in his place. You can't focus properly when a counter Press Conference is being held outside the hall where you are holding your meting.

AFP   Do you mean the meeting outside is a counter Press Conference?

AP   We'll soon find out. Let's go.

[They all leave the way they came in through the front entrance which leads to the foreground and garden where the public seems to be having a whale of fun. The cameras begin panning on the central figure of the extraordinary event that interrupted a presidential Press Conference. That interruption is in itself remarkable and one can imagine the news headlines that will come *out of these contradictory events. The central figure is our friend Zegonfo II who is dressed in the same garb we saw him last time with the addition that he now has a bullhorn to which he is speaking. He is surrounded, as though by prior arrangement, by hundreds of women dressed in white native costumes and carrying palm leaves in celebration of Easter. The women repeat words of incantation in response to his incantation.]*

ZEGONFO II	Kiraraiso!
WOMEN	Kiraraiso.
ZEGONFO II	Lord have mercy on us for the sake of Mary
WOMEN	Have mercy on us, Oh Christ.

[This continues for several minutes]

ZEGONFO II   Hear me, people of Asmara,

I have come to bury the past, not resurrect it.

The noble President has told you that I am here to depose him.

If it were so, may the bones of my father,

sharpened to the point of the lance,

pierce me through the heart, and may I drop dead therefrom.

BBC   This man must be literate in English literature. He is paraphrasing Shakespeare's Julius Caesar. I know the local language fairly well and I can tell you he is conversant with English literature.

AP   Ya, but what I want to know is, to what end is all this speech? Why is he dressed exotically like this? Who is this man?

[Before the BBC man could answer, Zegonfo II continues to harangue his audience.]

ZEGONFO II   I do not covet my neighbor's job, nor his wife, nor his servant.

My kingdom is not of this world. But my eyes have seen the misery of the multitude, and my ears have heard tales of woe that should put to shame anyone in power responsible for the welfare of the people.

I cannot keep silent when I see and hear injustice in a land whose heroes fell fighting for justice.

[Loud cheers and applause].

BBC	The words flow from him as they would from the old prophets. And he alternates between Shakespeare and the Bible.
AP	What did he say just now, that drew the cheer?
BBC	I'll tell you later. Oh My! I think the security are coming in full force to arrest him. Look.

[Lo! and behold, a number of plain-clothes men descend upon the scene, followed by armed, uniformed police. The police start fanning out around the crowd and pushing and shoving the women surrounding Zegonfo II. When the women see the uniformed police, they rush to Zegonfo's rescue, cutting the police off by forming a human wall of several dozen of them who throw themselves at the ring some lying on the ground, others locking arms in rings of three circles around the intended police target. A scuffle ensues in which some of the police use their batons to strike at some of the women, breaking the first ring. No sooner is a ring broken than another one is formed by more women rushing to fill in the gap, thus trapping the police inside a human cordon. All of a sudden, a hail-storm of stones begin falling on the police who are not wearing helmets. Some of them are injured which frightens the rest. It slackens their ability to concentrate on Zegonfo II, as they are pushed further out of the ring by women. Meanwhile, as Zegonfo counsels a peaceful end to the incident, the cameramen of the foreign press are rolling their cameras, having a time of their life. To the foreign press this seems to be more headline catching than any presidential press conference.]

ZEGONFO II	My good people. Women of Asmara. I don't want any bloodshed. No one must be harmed on my account. If there is to be any harm, let it fall upon my head. And I am ready for it. Greater people than me, like my fellow freedom fighter, Dr. Senai, have fallen victim to injustice. We do not know what has happened to him and his likes. They spoke the truth. And the truth which is the most potent liberating force, caused their imprisonment. The truth should set people free, not cause their imprisonment. But such is the irony of life in our poor nation. Mind you, this is the sacrifice from which redemption will come sooner or later. There can be no redemption without sacrifice. Have no fear. Be bold, be valiant, be strong.

A WOMAN LEADER	We shall be strong, Zegonfo, have no fear. Our children have not paid their dues in blood for nothing. Our husbands have not toiled for nothing. Zegonfo, we shall be strong and we love you, oh messenger of peace and good tidings.
ZEGONFO II	And now I want to address a few words of admonition to the police and the powers behind them who have disturbed this peaceful demonstration, this exercise of constitutional right.
WOMAN	Forget the police. They swore to uphold justice, but have become instruments of injustice.
ZEGONFO II	Be charitable as the Good Book teaches. They have families; they have rents to pay, mouths to feed. They obey orders because they must. But a time will come when they too will stand squarely on the side of justice. Give them time.
WOMAN	How long, Zegonfo, how long? It has been ten years.
ZEGONFO II	Have you heard of the story of Saul? He was the chief guard who used to persecute Christians. One day, when he was traveling on the road to Damascus, the Lord appeared to him and asked him, "Saul, Saul, why do you persecute me?" From then on, the arch persecutor, the chief of police of the time, became a great preacher. He became Saint Paul, the great apostle. So don't give up on the police; they will see the light one day, soon.

[Added to the shower of stones, Zegonfo's admonition seems to calm the police. The stone throwers also seem to have ceased their activities as if they are in league with the spirit that moves this strange figure, called Zegonfo II. But as he starts walking away from the palace ground, his women guards walk encircling him, some of them warning the police off.] |
THE WOMAN LEADER	[Addressing a police officer] If you people are thinking of arresting Zegonfo, there will be bloodshed and let that blood be on your heads.
POLICE OFFICER	We have orders to arrest him.
WOMAN	On what grounds
POLICE	On the ground of public disturbance, of organizing an unlawful meeting.
WOMAN	There was no disturbance until you came. This was a peaceful and lawful meeting. It is a meeting guaranteed

	by our Constitution. Are you above the Constitution, officer?
POLICE	No I am not, but the law tells me to follow superior orders.
WOMAN	Would you kill a human being just because your superior officer tells you to kill in a peaceful situation?
POLICE	No, but I am not proposing to kill this man, I am proposing to arrest him in accordance with the order issued by the government.

[*The efforts of the police to carry out the order for Zegonfo's arrest is also complicated by the fact that the whole place has become a scene of attraction to the populace. It looks as if the entire inhabitants of the city have heard the excitement and stopped their work to come and witness this extraordinary event. As for the foreign press, their cameramen must be exhausted filming all aspects of the exciting event. The chief of the security and the police must have been given an order to cease and desist from carrying out the plan of arrest, because they are starting to leave the scene. Accordingly, Zengofo, surrounded by his feminine entourage begins his exit from the scene. As he walks people clear the way. It is as if the Red Sea is opening once more.*]

ZEGONFO II	Praised be the Lord!
SOME FROM THE CROWD	Amen!
ZEGONFO II	[*Waving to the applauding Crowd*] My eyes have seen the glory of the Lord. The police have been reduced to lambs, like the lions in Daniel's den.
CROWD	Amen.
A PRESSMAN	Whereto now Zegonfo II? Where will you spend the night? Are you not concerned that the police will pick you up from your house?
ZEGONFO II	My house is with the dead. Tonight, I shall tell my fallen comrades that the voice of the weak prevailed over that of the strong. The weak have become strong. The fools have become wise, as it was written.
AP	What do you mean, your house is with the dead?
ZEGONFO II	It is not possible for you to understand. You have to make commitment to die in order to understand what I am talking about. I am with the dead. Although I am

	in this world, I am not of this world. You come from a culture which makes living for material comfort a civic virtue. I grew up in a culture that teases and mocks death.
BBC	[*To AP*] I will explain to you who he is and what all this means when we go back to our hotel. I think we have seen and heard enough.
AP	I could not have enough of this man. I hope we can catch him tomorrow or the day after, if they don't arrest him.
BBC	They won't, he is elusive. Don't be fooled by his apparent simplicity. He was a freedom fighter, a guerilla fighter that is, and he can elude them provided the public can give him safe conduct from here.
AP	Is that likely?
BBC	I think so.

[*Zegonfo disappears into the crowd. The BBC journalist is approached by a woman shrouded in the white native sheet—the same woman who was quizzing the police officer. She has been following him from a safe distance, as he followed Zegonfo's slow march towards the exit of the palace garden. As soon as she comes closer to him, she uncovers her face. It is Sister Delores. The BBC man is surprised to find that a woman who is dressed like an ordinary "native" could have such command of English.*]

SISTER DELORES	Will you give the event good coverage?
BBC	You can bet your sweet head we will.
SISTER DELORES	[*Looking around and whispering*] We want the world to know the truth, no more no less.
BBC	You speak in the plural "we," can I ask you who you are?
SISTER DELORES	Let us just say, I represent the silent majority, who need a voice. They are silent because they have been muzzled. Their only free press was abolished and its editors and reporters imprisoned. No one knows where they are or if they are alive.
BBC	Do you know any of their relatives? I want to interview them.
SISTER DELORES	Yes, I do. If you give me a day or two, I can arrange for you to meet some of them.

BBC	Are you a member of some underground movement?
SISTER DELORES	You might say that.
BBC	I would like to interview you, using an assumed name. Would you grant me that?
SISTER DELORES	I will do better than that; I will take you to one of the leaders of the undergeound. Also, the BBC should contact the foreign representatives of the underground. Some of them are members of our leadership, you know.
BBC	I will try. But that happens to be not in my area of coverage; mine is East Africa. But I'll pass your information to those who cover Europe. By the way, where did you learn to speak such good English?
SISTER DELORES	[*Coyly giggling*] Oh, here and there. Which hotel are you staying in?
BBC	At the Hamasien.
SISTER DELORES	Some one will contact you posing as a travel agent and he will take you to a secret place for the interview. It will probably be in the evening between seven and nine. Is that okay?
BBC	Yes it is. And thank you.
SISTER DELORES	Good bye for now.
BBC	Cheerio.

SCENE FOUR

[*The Cathedral of Asmara. On a bright sunny day in June. On the steps of the front entrance of the cathedral, a young man is pacing slowly to and fro, along the top step. He is dressed in jeans trousers and green jacket. He is also wearing a sports cap and sun glasses and, although it is a warm windless day, he has his jacket collars turned up which makes him stand out with an odd appearance. It may be for that reason that someone has his binoculars trained on him from a hotel room opposite the cathedral. There is rhythmic deliberateness in his steps indicating a man with a mission. Whether his mission has to do with the religion associated with the building at whose doors he is strutting will be soon revealed.*

When he is about to enter the cathedral, he is greeted by two young men his age who seem to know him by sight, but obviously not that well, because they don't stop to talk to him. One of them is thin and tall, the other is fat and short. They move past him further up the steps, standing a few step above him but within hearing distance. They continue their conversation, all the while the fat man keeping a look-out for him, from time to time. Our mysterious man thus decides to wait, listening to their conversation.]

THIN MAN	I still don't agree with you that Zegonfo is play-acting and that he is sane. Did you hear him the other day at the Palace ground, saying he is not from this world? What does that tell you about his sanity?
FAT MAN	It tells me that he is devilishly clever, or angelically clever, depending on whether you look upon him with favor or not. Did you notice how he brought the name of Dr. Senai in the midst of a long harangue about injustice in this country. That was a clever way of telling the public about the opposition movement.
THIN MAN	He knew him during the war of liberation. Mad people don't forget the past and their friends from the past.
FAT MAN	I say he is as sane as you and me, but perhaps cleverer. I never thought I would live to see the day when a cleverer man than you would appear. [*He laughs voluptuously from down his guts and pats the thin man on the back*]. Sorry. That just came out of me. I didn't intend it, but it is true. [*More laughter*].
THIN MAN	Laughter comes easily to fat men. I envy you.
FAT MAN	Don't envy me. If ability to laugh easily comes only with fatness, then you don't want it, my friend. But to come back to the Zegonfo riddle, I have a theory that I want to try.
THIN ME	What is that
FAT MAN	Well, let's assume that he is pretending to be mad but is, in fact, part of an underground movement.
THIN MAN	All right.
FAT MAN	I know where he spends the night because I have a cousin who is with the secret service of the government. My cousin is supposed to report to the security office about Zegonfo's hiding place, but does not tell because he is in sympathy with the underground movement.
THIN MAN	If your cousin is keeping Zegonfo's hiding place secret, he obviously suspects Zegonfo to be a member of the underground movement.
FAT MAN	He told me so himself and I am telling you this in confidence.
THIN MAN	So what is your theory.

FAT MAN	I want to meet him in secret and tell him I am a member of the underground, feed some genuine information about the movement and see what he says.
THIN MAN	What if he does not respond as you think he will? What is the use of such an exercise. In what way will it help the cause?
FAT MAN	You know me, I am a curious animal. The cause is one thing, and I support it. But a bit of adventure on the side won't hurt anybody.
THIN MAN	You must have been reading some mystery novels or watching detective movies.
FAT MAN	[*Laughing*] I am curious by nature and don't need detective novels to excite my imagination. You get your thrill may be doing that. I get my thrill getting into situations like the one I am proposing to do.
THIN MAN	Well, leave me out of it. What we have been doing is dangerous enough. It is one thing to be caught acting for a cause, but getting caught on a thrill exercise is ridiculous.
FAT MAN	It is the same thing when you come right down to it. Some get their thrill doing drugs, others getting involved in underground movements.
THIN MAN	Is that what you think of our involvement with the cause of justice and democracy?
FAT man	Don't get me wrong. I believe in the cause. But I think I am being intellectually honest when I say that being a member of an underground movement has its thrills. To put it another way, the thrill is the frill of the cause. [*Laughter*].
THIN MAN	It is not funny.
FAT man	[*Laughing more loudly*] You need to relax my friend. Why shouldn't fighting for a cause be fun. You should enjoy what you do. If you enjoy it, you will be good at it. *Capisci?*
THIN MAN	I do enjoy what I do, and I need no frills, thank you.
FAT man	You are a hopeless puritan. Beware of puritans! Do you know the definition of a Puritan?

[*At this point, our mysterious man moves closer to the two men and sit on the steps, putting his chin on the up-turned palms of hi hands, so that no one can recognize him. The fat man draws closer to his thin companion and speaks in barely audible whispers.*

The mysterious man realizes this and pretends to look away.]

THIN MAN	He may be one of them.
FAT MAN	Could be, but he didn't hear us. He couldn't have heard us; we were not speaking that loudly.

[Two men dressed casually in khaki appear on the scene. One of them stops near the chatting friends; the other stops at the foot of the cathedral steps. At this point the mysterious man gets up and walks slowly up toward the cathedral entrance. The new arrival at the bottom of the steps moves up with quickening steps and stops when the mysterious man turns round to see him. The mysterious man paces along the top platform leading to the entrance. After a few minutes of pacing on the platform, he looks at his watch and continues pacing for a couple of more minutes, looks around surveying the road across and enters the cathedral.

The cathedral pews are almost empty. Only a couple of elderly people are sitting in the middle, fingering their beads and murmuring words of prayers. The mysterious young man walks along the left aisle of the cathedral towards the confessional. He hears voices coming from beyond the altar, on the left side, and moves closer to where the voice came from. The voices continue in a low murmur; he cannot make out their words but distinguishes a male and a female voice. He had seen two people –a man and a woman—enter the cathedral by the side door, before he came round to the front entrance.

"I was right," he murmurs to himself. As he goes closer he realizes the voices come from the sacristy. He hears footsteps from the direction of the cathedral entrance and sits on one of the pews and lowers his head until it disappears. A voice comes booming from the sacristy.]

MALE VOICE	Who is there? Is anybody there?

[The steps cease; the intruder dives beside the pew on the right aisle]. It must be somebody outside. There is no one here.

FEMALE VOICE	No one except the priest comes as far as here. Don't worry, but lower your voice. What I fear most is the possibility of a priest coming in here.

MALE VOICE	The more dangerous it is the more excited I become. It has always been like that with me the more risk, the more thrilling. That is why I accepted your idea of meeting here.
FEMALE VOICE	Don't you care for your reputation?
MALE VOICE	I used to; not any more. Now tell me, why did you ask for an assignation here?
FEMALE VOICE	Assignation? Why this is about a subject of mutual interest. But I chose this place because I suspected you might find it intriguing to meet in a church. You have never done that-meet in a church for political discussions, I mean. My insight into your character from past observation is that you enjoy taking risks.
MALE VOICE	That's true. So now what are you proposing? Your message said you had an urgent business. I hoped it might include discussion about a new assignment for you, that you have reconsidered our offer for you to work for us.
FEMALE VOICE	There are many things we need to discuss. *[Suddenly alarmed]* I hear voices from the side doors; that is the entrance of the priest. We better make sure no one is coming. *[The voices cease]* Our meeting may be misunderstood and given a wrong interpretation. What with your reputation nowadays!
MALE VOICE	What do you mean my reputation nowadays?

[As he comes closer to the sacristy, the young man recognizes the male voice which confirms his suspicion and rewards his painstaking pursuit. He stands up from the pew, surveys the interior of the cathedral and, seeing no one, walks slowly towards the sacristy. As he walks surreptitiously, cat's paw fashion, the man hiding on the right aisle gets up and moves fast forward toward the right side of the altar. The mysterious man takes off his cap and sun-glasses and pulls out a gun out of his jacket pocket. Then he runs towards the sacristy and shouts.]

"You son of a bitch, you must die! You must die if the nation is to live."

[He fires two shots. The shots shatter a table and the intended target dives behind the table. He fires two more shots, again missing the target].

THE FEMALE VOICE	No, Yikalo, no!

[Yikalo fires again his last shot but obviously misses. In the meantime the man who was on the right aisle has run forward and fires three shots from an automatic gun, fatally wounding Yikalo who falls gasping for air. His last words to the female whose voice now has a face are.]

Sister Delores, this is the only way.

SISTER DELORES   *[Holding the dying Yikalo in her arms]* Oh, Yikalo, Yikalo! What have you done? Oh you poor boy, you desperate boy! What have you done?

[The target gets up from behind the desk and stands above the shaken Sister Delores and motions the man who shot Yikalo to come forward, pats him on the back and whispers something in his ears. The man goes out of the cathedral comes back with two other men. One of them takes out handcuffs and puts it round Sister Delores' wrists and yanks her up. She is dazed but not weeping. She looks at the intended target who grins at her.]

HE   You must see the irony of it all, Yikalo killed by a Warsay.

SISTER DELORES   He was Yikalo in name only; his father is the real Yikalo and you have locked him up, or may be killed him.

HE   You took me for a fool. I knew you had something up your sleeves, when you asked for an appointment in church. My men have been following your steps ever since I got word that you held a meeting in the chapel of your Mission.

SISTER DELORES   Do you know what you are? You are the devil incarnate.

HE   And what are you, a saint?

SISTER DELORES   No, I am just an unworthy servant of the Lord, trying to do good, trying to help people in need. But if it comes to that I am ready to meet any suffering for a just cause.

HE   Are you willing to go to the length that Yikalo, here, has gone? You say you are trying to help people in need. What was Yikalo in need of, I wonder? Wait, don't tell me. He was in need of justice and democracy, the catchwords of Western governments who are trying to tell us how to run our affairs. And you decided you could help him and others to get justice and democracy. Well, I got news for you and other do-gooders. Our people already have justice and democracy.

SISTER DELORES	Tell me, is it just to lock up people without trial and deny their families access to them? Is it just to send twenty thousand young men and women to their deaths on an ill-conceived and ill-prepared war? And is it democratic to do that without consulting the peoples' representatives?
HE	I'll ignore your questions, which are based on the false claims of defeatists and traitors. What our people need most are bread and housing and roads and hospitals, and we are doing our best to provide them with that. We will not be intimidated by threats and blackmails of your European masters.
SISTER DELORES	I have but one master to whom I am betrothed, and He will, in His own good time, throw you out like the rest of Africa's tyrants.
HE	Has he told you that? Did you also contact him before you decided to meet me in his house, and did you tell him to bless you or excuse you for the sacrilege?
SISTER DELORES	Sacrilege! What do you know about sacrilege? You know nothing about sacrilege. Murder is the worst kind of offence against God and man.
HE	*[His temper rising]* Are you accusing me of murder?
SISTER DELORES	I hope some one else will some day soon.
HE	*[Indignant and at the top of his voice]* Take her away. Get her out of my sight and lock her up. No, take her to the investigation room and report to me by tonight what story she will tell by the end of the interrogation.
THE SECURITY MAN	What shall we do with the corpse?
HE	Take it to the morgue. First order a hospital ambulance and tell them to park on the side entrance of the cathedral. Tell the police to cordon off the area. Later in the day, you may send for some relative of their family and tell him to inform the mother. Write the usual police report on the incident and send me the first draft. No one else is to know before I read the first draft. Understood?
THE MAN	Yes sir.
	[There is a knock at the side door, which the security man had locked. A shout of "Open the door, this is the Cathedral Administrator" is heard, as Sister Delores is taken out by the side door into a waiting police car. The Boss also leaves, using the same side entrance door. As she leaves the cathedral, she stops and turns towards the Boss.]

SISTER DELORES	May misfortune pursue you all the days of your life. And may you rot in hell!
THE BOSS	How unkind of you! What happened to your Christian charity?
SISTER DELORES	You think you know everything, don't you? Well, even the devil can quote Scriptures. And I know I will be forgiven for this sin. Will you be forgiven for all the mortal sins and crimes you have committed? May the Lord forgive me for saying so, but I doubt if people like you will be forgiven. There must be a special place in hell for people like you!

[The Boss responds with a staccato laughter, as Sister Delores is taken away. Outside the cathedral a crowd had started gathering. Among them are the fat short man and his tall, thin companion.]

FAT MAN	*[Whispering to the thin man and pointing to Sister Delores]* Who is this woman and why is she being taken handcuffed?
THIN MAN	I have seen her many times. She is a catholic nun. But, like you, I don't know why they are arresting her.

[More police arrive at the scene and an ambulance is seen approaching on the western side of the cathedral. One policeman comes to wards the crowd and tells them to disperse. Two others place two movable poles and tie yellow cords on them blocking entrance to the street on the western side road. Two men come out of an ambulance vehicle carrying a stretcher and enter the cathedral.]

THIN MAN	Somebody is hurt, the shots we heard must have been from real live ammunition.
FAT MAN	But shooting in the cathedral! And a nun being arrested! This is intriguing.
THIN MAN	Yes, the plot thickens. We better leave before some one arrests us.
FAT MAN	Why would they arrest us?
THIN MAN	I don't know. I just feel a sense of danger. Let's go. *[He turns to leave].*
FAT MAN	Wait, some one is coming out of the cathedral. Santa Madonna! It is the Almighty One. What the hell is he doing here? The plot is indeed thickening and I'll be damned if I leave the scene as it becomes so interesting. You go if you want.

THIN MAN	Okay I'll stay, but if we are arrested, I will curse you. You know I have black spots on my tongue, so my curse works.
FAT MAN	We won't be arrested. Our cell is secure, no one knows what we have been doing. Don't worry.
	[The Boss walks down the cordoned side door and disappears behind the rear end of the cathedral and the two friends begin walking away from the crowd, which has started thinning in response to the order of the police.]
FAT MAN	Why are you so worried? First of all, no one will arrest us. Even if they arrest us, and we begin to spill the beans, they will have to arrest half of the adult population that is organized in the underground movement. They don't have prison facilities to accommodate all these people.
THIN MAN	Do you think they care about that? They'll just build a concentration camp and surround it with barbed wire. All they need then is a handful of armed guards.
	[The two friends disappear into the wider avenue, as the ambulance car passes by blowing the siren sound and people go about their daily business as if nothing happened.]

SCENE FIVE

[A week later. At the Interrogation Center of the Special Security. It is the same place where the sudden death of Teklu and Manna occurred. The office has been improved somewhat, in view of the visit of the Boss, which happens from time to time, whenever there is a special inmate. This is one of those times. The Boss had arrived, heavily escorted by several cars and was welcomed by Teklu's successor, Andu, ever eager to outdo his late predecessor in pleasing the Boss. To that career-advancing objective, Andu ordered a large picture of the Boss to be placed on the wall behind his desk as well as the walls behind the desks of all section heads of the Security Department. He also adorned the room with various pictures depicting Eritrean life. Placed in a particularly prominent place is a picture of the Boss in his heyday as a tegadalai, looking gentle and amiable.]

BOSS	*[Walking round the room and surveying the room's contents with a disconcerting grimace at everything, including his own picture]* Where is she now?
ANDU	She is in the interrogation room, sir.
BOSS	Do you have her file?
ANDU	Yes, sir. *[He opens one of the drawers, takes out a brown-colored file and hands it to him].*

BOSS	*[Taking a seat in one of the chairs, starts reading, flipping the pages of the file]* I'll take this home and read it. Meanwhile, give me a summary of the testimony.
ANDU	She admitted that she belongs to an underground movement.
BOSS	What else?
ANDU	She admires Dr. Senai and the other traitors.
BOSS	*[With growing impatience]* Details, details! I want details. Did you discover any weakness in her character or background that we can use to induce her cooperation?
ANDU	She is very stubborn, sir, very defiant.
BOSS	Stubborn! Defiant! Didn't you use force?
ANDU	No sir.
BOSS	Why not?
ANDU	You told me, "No force is to be used on her, sir."
BOSS	*[Gets up and slaps Andu]* When did I tell you that?
ANDU	*[Visibly stunned by the Boss's sudden resort to violence about which he had heard but not seen until this minute]* You phoned me the evening of the day she was arrested. You said "Don't use any force on her." *[Intimidated by the menacing look of the Boss and, in a reverse apology typical of an ambitious but servile mind, he adds]*. You were busy sir, so you must have forgotten.
BOSS	Never mind, never mind. But you could have used the threat of violence, which is sometimes as effective as its use. Didn't they teach you that at the Zero school?
ANDU	No sir, but I was going to mention something, before you slapped me, which may give a key to certain weakness.
BOSS	What is it?
ANDU	Well, she was recently reunited with a younger sister. She seems to be very fond of this sister and very protective.
BOSS	That's more like it. And how do you propose to use that fact
ANDU	Our secret agents have been trailing her sister. She is a university student who has done her service at Sawa, and is highly critical of the Sawa military commanders.
BOSS	Why? What does she say?

ANDU	She talks about rapes in the camps and in the trenches. She speaks of forced pregnancies.
BOSS	[*With an ironic twist in his voice*] Well, what else is new! I send a thousand women and they come back doubling their number. Now what use have you made of the information of her sister when interrogating her?
ANDU	I haven't yet. But I am working on it.
BOSS	Okay, let's leave that for now. What else?
ANDU	Before she became a nun, she studied history in Ireland; she has a Masterate in history.
BOSS	What about her relation to our struggle?
ANDU	She boasted of having risked her life several times for the cause of Eritrean liberation. She did not want to elaborate. So, we think she is just trying to gain our favor by pretending to be a *tegadalit*.
BOSS	Wrong. She did take risks—huge risks.
ANDU	[*Contrite*] Sorry, sir; I didn't know?
BOSS	Of course you didn't. How could you? You were sheltered in the safe quarters at the head office.
ANDU	[*Sotto voce*] So were you.
BOSS	What was that?
ANDU	I said, "how right you are, sir."
BOSS	All right, I want to see her. Go and fetch her.
	[*Andu leaves and after a couple of minutes brings in Sister Delores who is dressed in the simple Khaki uniform worn by prisoners. He gets out of the room, leaving her face to face with the Boss. They stand facing each other for a moment, without uttering a word.*]
BOSS	[*Smiles at her and motions to the chair on her right as he sits down behind the desk on Andu's chair*] Sit down, won't you?
SISTER DELORES	I prefer to stand thank you. And to what do I owe the honor of this visit?
BOSS	I have come to take you out for dinner.
SISTER DELORES	[*Startled but incredulous*] Where, to the Shamrock?
BOSS	I must say, for a woman of the cloth, you have a foul mouth.

SISTER DELORES	Could it be because I am not wearing the right cloth; as you can see, I am wearing the prison overalls. They have de-robbed me of my nun's habit, robbing me of my religious right.
BOSS	*[With his eyes scouring up and down her entire body, lasciviously]* I see what you mean. Actually, the prison outfit becomes you. It resonates with your vow of poverty and humility.
SISTER DELORES	*[Ignoring his comment and lascivious look]* If you have any influence with the prison warden, tell him to return my nun's habit.
BOSS	*[Annoyed]* If I have what?
SISTER DELORES	Yes, if you have influence. The warden is a close friend of yours, I am told. If you only knew what goes on inside the prison.
BOSS	How do you know? You've only been detained for a week. And what do you mean, if I only knew? Of course I know.
SISTER DELORES	I doubt it. Even though you are a dictator, I have a feeling you would not countenance what goes on inside the prison, if you knew. You care about your reputation too much to allow it, despite your pretence not to care.
BOSS	*[Suddenly rising and coming round the desk to come closer to her]*Ok I'll order them to give you back your nun's habit. *[Boss uses the intercom to summon Andu who arrives within two minutes. Andu salutes.]*
BOSS	Take the prisoner away and bring her back in her nun's habit. Pronto.
ANDU	*[Salutes]* Right away Sir. *[Take Sister Delores away and brings her back dressed in her habit. Salutes and from the room.]*
BOSS	I am not sure now whether you look more beautiful in your habit or in the Prison uniform. Any way, enough of your sarcasm. Let us talk about more pleasant subjects.
SISTER DELORES	Like what?
BOSS	Like food. Have you had dinner?
SISTER DELORES	Oh yes. I had a banquet consisting of an entree of oysters and salad. For the main dish they gave me choice New York Strip. For dessert…
BOSS	Come on, be serious. I meant it when I told you I came to take you out to dinner.

SISTER DELORES	Do you think you can tempt me with food, because I have been deprived of it for a week?
BOSS	Sister Delores, believe me, I have no ulterior motives. I have come to take you out to dinner. No hidden agenda, I just want to talk to you.
SISTER DELORES	Why? What do you want to talk about?
BOSS	You intrigue me. Ever since the cathedral incident last week and your idea of holding a meeting with me at a Catholic shrine, I have been asking myself, why did she want to meet there? What is she up to? Then of course there is the fact of your involvement in the underground movement in association with traitors. Why should a Catholic nun do all this?
SISTER DELORES	[Smiling for the first time] The Devil made me do it.
BOSS	[Playing along with a smile] Hey, the Devil is a friend of mine. He couldn't have set you against me. If I may change the subject, has your younger sister been here to see you?
SISTER DELORES	[Looking alarmed] What do you know about my sister, and why are you asking this question? What have you done with her?
BOSS	Relax, nothing has happened to your sister. Don't worry, nothing will happen to her. But I am thinking of recalling all Sawa servicemen and women to do a different kind of national service. What is your sister's name, I becoming forgetful; getting old I suppose.
SISTER DELORES	Her name is Saba. [She studies his face for any hint of his intentions].
BOSS	Oh, yes, Saba. She is studying in the University, I know and has been to Sawa. My next move is to create a Yikalo/Warsay national service, dedicated to a speedy and radical transformation of this society. I will begin experimenting with the Summer-time volunteer service of youth brigades.
SISTER DELORES	The kind of volunteer service in which two students died last year?
BOSS	That was an unfortunate incident, but the student brought it on themselves. These pampered skunks have to be taught a lesson, have to be disciplined. I am determined to create a new generation of Eritreans devoid of the old sentiments and sentimentalities. I am

going to create a new breed of Eritreans. I will succeed where others failed, and nothing is going to stop me.

[Sister Delores studies him closely, perceiving, for the first time, in the flushed face and the strange outburst of arrogance and ambition, the external manifestation of a deranged mind. Even his strange offer to take her to dinner from a jail cell is indicative of such state of mind. So she prepares herself for the worst.]

SISTER DELORES   This incredibly crazy idea will fail; it will fail just like all the others. Our humane traditions and religions will defeat your crazy scheme. You ordered innocent young kids to stand in the scorching heat of the desert and did not bat an eye when two of them died.

BOSS   It is not true, I sent messages of condolences to the parents and ordered an investigation. These things happen. It is part of the struggle. You must understand that.

SISTER DELORES   No I don't understand that. Nor do I understand why you ordered a unit of the army to shoot and kill disabled veterans when they tried to come to Asmara to make a peaceful demonstration.

BOSS   That was an unfortunate accident. It should not have happened and I did not order them to shoot and kill.

SISTER DELORES   Then why did you reward the officer who ordered the shooting with a special appointment as head of an important army unit?

BOSS   *[Shifting in his seat and getting frustrated]* You think you know everything, don't you?

SISTER DELORES   No, you think you know everything. You have been acting like God, omnipresent and omniscient.

BOSS   What a pity. An intelligent woman like you and a Catholic nun at that falling under the influence of bad guys. I wonder what your mother superior will think of this? By the way, she was expelled from the country because she was found interfering in our politics. It looks as if the entire Catholic establishment has risen against us. I wonder what we have done to deserve that. To come back to your sister's case, did they tell you that she might be taken in for questioning?

[He stopped to watch her reaction as she also scrutinized his face. This mutual scrutiny of two inscrutable faces went on for a few seconds, as they silently observed each

other in surreptitious glances. Finally, she spoke doing
her utmost not to reveal any anxiety and thus give him
an advantage in this mental game—in this contest of
wills, one politically motivated, the other spiritually
fortified.]

SISTER DELORES   No, they didn't tell me whoever it is that you are
referring to.

BOSS   That's odd. I am referring to my people here, of course.
It looks as if they have been soft on you, and lenient.
Do you mean to tell me they did not tell you that we
suspect her of being a messenger between the arch
traitor, Woldu and the Weyane?

SISTER DELORES   You are bluffing. I know my sister is not capable of doing
what you just said she did. You are trying to soften me
and make me do whatever it is you want. If you want
to know what I have been involved in all you have to
do is read the file. I have nothing to add to that. You
added one more wrong to your mountain of wrongs
in expelling Sister Maria Emma. She is innocent of any
blame. I broke my vows and the rules of the Order in
getting involved in politics, against her strict orders and
without her knowledge.

BOSS   What about her statement that she supports the
European Union's demarche against us?

SISTER DELORES   I know nothing about that and I don't believe it. All I
know is that she gave us all strict orders to respect the law
and policies of this country. She couldn't have expressed
any opinion on the European Union's demarche even if
she may secretly agree with it. As for your claim that the
Catholic establishment is working against you, nothing
can be further from the truth. On the contrary, I have
an ax to grind with them for being too much on the side
of the established order, even when the order is against
democracy and justice, as yours is.

[*Unable to control himself, he rises from his chair and
advances towards her and tries to grab her. She ducks
and runs round the desk yelling "Help!"*]

BOSS   [*Running after her and trying to remove the chair which
she pushed to block him*] There is no help for you here.
Let Him whose spouse you claim to be come down and
help you.

SISTER DELORES   Help me, Sweet Jesus!

BOSS	[Laughing hysterically and grabbing the top part of the chair and pulling it away] That's right, call him. [She cries "Help! Help!] Well, where is he? Where is your precious Lord? Come on now, let's be reasonable. If you act reasonably and accept my offers and solicitations, I will not only be lenient with you, but I will spare your sister the agony of detention and worse things. I hear she is a lovely girl. What do you say?
SISTER DELORES	You are bluffing; my sister is an innocent girl who is a good student.
BOSS	[Chasing her round the desk] What does it matter if she is innocent or not? If I say she is guilty, she is guilty. Now be sensible. Let me take you out to dinner in a nice place.
SISTER DELORES	Never!
HE	[Leapfrogs the desk and grabs her by the shoulder and pulls her toward him. She struggles trying to disentangle herself and bites his hand. He slaps her twice.
	She is dazed but fights back, kicking him in the shin. He knocks her down unconscious. Turning towards the sleeping beauty and looking at her with a softened visage, curiously studies the pretty face of this woman who has intrigued him.]
BOSS	You foolish woman, foolish and nosy. Why did you have to meddle in this dangerous game? Why did you have to fall among a crowd of traitors? I could give you the world had you asked for it. We could have done great things together. What am I going to do with you? Your stubborn belief and martyrdom complex will bring tons of trouble, and I am already troubled. Whatever I do seems to go wrong. [Rising and hardening with a lump in his voice, and striking a heroic mode] No, I will not relent. Let them say what they want. I am the progeny of two Woldenkiels. I will not be seen as weak, if hell freezes over. I will not relent. I will not. I WILL NOT!

[Sister Delores wakes and springs up standing upright. Before she could move away around the desk, he grabs her and tries to pull her skirt up over her head. As she resists, he grabs her underwear, trying to pull it out, succeeding to take it below her knees and exposing her private parts. Suddenly, she seems to be willing to submit to his will. She smiles at him and assumes the pose of a femme fatale. He seems confused and hesitates, when she plants a kiss smack on his lips. As he relaxes and gently *holds her by the waist, she caresses his groin. This rouses him, he takes off his trousers, tears her underwear off her, pushes his knees between her legs and leans forward to rape her.*

Suddenly, she quickly gets hold of his testicles with her right hand and starts to squeeze them tightly causing him to emit a loud groan of excruciating pain. But somehow, he manages to get hold of her neck and starts squeezing it.]

BOSS A....gh! I will strangle you to death, you bitch! A..... agh!!!

SISTER DELORES Not before I turn you into a eunuch, you murderer!

[So the femme fatale *pose was a ruse born of desperation. And they are enfolded in a deadly embrace—she squeezing harder and harder with every once of her strength—he squeezing her neck with all his superior force. Their mutually inflicted pain becomes the source of agonizing groans from both of them. Who will give in?]*

* * * * *

[Five days later at Andu's home. The thin, tall man and fat, short man just entered the house and are being seated by Andu, who is the short fat man's cousin.]

SHORT FAT MAN *[Addressing Andu and introducing his friend]* Andu, I have told you about my friend who has been eager to meet you for quite a while.

ANDU Yes, you have told me many times. I am glad to meet him. *[Addressing thin man]* Welcome to my humble home.

THIN, TALL MAN Thank you. I am curious to know many things, but I have been particularly intrigued by the story, of a Catholic nun who was arrested about two weeks ago from the Cathedral.

ANDU Yes, she has been nothing but trouble for some of us. Thank God, she is no longer a problem.

THIN MAN How so?

ANDU Because she is no longer alive.

THIN MAN She is dead?

ANDU Yes, I'd say, very dead

THIN MAN How did she die?

ANDU	Ambition caused her death. She tried to wrestle against God, so to speak, like Jacob in the Bible.
SHORT MAN	*[Chuckling mischievously]* Come on cousin, don't beat about the bush. Tell us the real story the truth, the whole truth, and nothing but the truth. It is all in the public domain now; no need to hide things.
THIN MAN	I have it from the grape vines that she was engaged in a tussle with the Boss. By the way, how is he?
ANDU	He is alive.
SHORT MAN	But alive with diminished manhood. *[He let out a loud laughter]*.
THIN MAN	Is he in the country?
ANDU	No, he is in Qatar undergoing medical treatment. But is okay, he will survive. This too shall pass.
SHORT MAN	Yes, but he lost his vital manhood, his virility. He is half the man he was, isn't he?
ANDU	*[Alarmed]* I don't know what you are talking about. You better watch your mouth, cousin. I will not be able to save you from Ear Earo, if you keep talking like that.

[Enter Zegonfo, with his Hermit's attire]

ANDU	*[Surprised]* What the hell are you doing here? Who showed you my house? How did you...
ZEGONFO II	Don't worry, Andu. No one knows I am here. As to how I came here, I am like the wind; I am everywhere. I have eyes and ears in places even you the spy master of the dictator would not suspect.
SHORT MAN	Merhaba Zeghie. And what brings you to my cousin's humble home?
ZEGONFO II	The same curiosity that brought you brought me here.
THIN MAN	And what are you curious to know?
ZEGONFO II	What happened at the police station five days ago is now the talk of town; it is part of the hideous story of our wounded nation. And I want to get to the bottom of it and exposed it to the world.
SHORT MAN	I am with you there brother. Let there be light! Let the light of public information shine on the dark corners of the bureaucracy!
ANDU	Shut up, or I'll arrest you for treason!

ZEGONFO II	The same way you arrested Dr. Senai and his comrades? The same way the dictator arrested the noble veterans who have disappeared?
ANDU	I can also arrest you, you fool.
ZEGONFO II	Yes you can, but I will slip through your bloody fingers like the fog of Nefasit. And before I do that, I will tell the story of the heroic Sister Delores who squeezed the vital life out of the dictator before he choked her to death. Because of her heroic act, the dictator is now half the man he was. Long live the memory of our martyrs. Sister Delores is one of our martyrs. May her memory be revered for ever. Say Amen!
THIN MAN AND SHORT MAN	Amen!

CURTAIN

THE END